Autism and the Seeds of Change

Autism and the Seeds of Change

Achieving Full Participation in Life through the Davis Autism Approach

Abigail Marshall

with

Ronald Dell Davis

ISBN-13: 978-1479373345

ISBN-10: 1479373346

Concept sequence and definitions, photographic images of clay models, and inverted pyramid graphic charts are ©Ronald Dell Davis

The terms Davis®, Davis Autism Approach®, Davis Orientation Counseling®, Davis Symbol Mastery®, and Davis Dyslexia Correction® are registered trademarks of Ronald D. Davis. Commercial use of these trademarks to identify educational, instructional, or therapeutic services requires licensing by the trademark owner.

Clay models and photos by Lorna Timms and Himi Ratnaka

Cover photo ©Vlad Mereuta—Fotolia.com

First Edition, October 2012.

Printed in the United States

Publisher's Cataloging-in-Publication data
Marshall, Abigail.
    Autism and the seeds of change : achieving full participation in life through the Davis autism approach / Abigail Marshall with Ronald Dell Davis.
    p. cm.
    ISBN 978-1479373345
    Includes bibliographical references.
1. Autism –Alternative Treatment. 2. Autism --Treatment. 3. Autism in children--Alternative treatment.4. Autistic children. I. Davis, Ronald D. (Ronald Dell), 1942-II. Title.
RC553.A88 M37 2012
616.85/882 --dc23   2012918016

*Dedicated to Dr. Fatima Ali, who was
there for us when the time was right*

Acknowledgements

The following Davis Facilitators have contributed to this book by sharing their insights and experiences gained from working with their clients.

Stacey Borger Smith	Calgary, Alberta, Canada
Cathy Cook	Columbia, Missouri, USA
Ray Davis	Burlingame, California, USA
Cathy Dodge Smith	Oakville, Ontario, Canada
Tina Guy	Nelson, New Zealand
Alma Holden	Alexandra, New Zealand
Gale Long	Elkview, West Virginia, USA
Marcia Maust	Berlin, Pennsylvania, USA
Cinda Osterman	Grand Ledge, Michigan, USA
Gabriela Scholter	Stuttgart, Germany
Elizabeth Currie Shier	Oakville, Ontario, Canada
Lawrence Smith, Jr.	Calgary, Alberta, Canada
Lorna Timms	Christchurch, New Zealand
Christien Vos	Groningen, Nederland
Yvonne Wong	Hong Kong, China

Table of Contents

Foreword

One day I met a beautiful young boy. He was eight years old; his parents had taken him out of school because, in his own words, he said, "I am so confused I am overwhelmed." They could see him closing down more and more each day. He asked me if I could help him and I said I would try.

It was not long before my heart began to sink as I realized for all of my willingness, determination, and skills I could not help him.

I was sitting across the table from a young boy who had the face of innocence, the smile of an angel and wisdom beyond his years, but was in a void.

I could reach into his void for a while and be with him, but I could not bring him along with me to participate in my world, the world where his family, friends and school were. That world was too overwhelming.

I turned to my mentor Ronald Davis for help, and he gave me a manuscript. It was a roadmap of how to help this young man. I was absorbed by each page; it all made sense, of course—why had I not thought this way before!

With Ron Davis' tutoring I was able to build on my previous experience with the Davis methods for dyslexia and attention deficits. My previous training and experience had given me the wisdom and most of the tools I needed, but Ron gave me the framework and guidance to be able to share these with a child who inhabited a different inner world. With the new approach, I saw this boy step out of his autistic world and walk alongside us in ours.

It was the most rewarding experience I ever had in all my years as an educator. From then on I felt compelled to continue this work. I was able to facilitate others like this young boy return to main-stream schools, move out of residential homes back to their families, gain employment and begin to have meaningful relationships. I was extremely satisfied.

However, it was not long before I realized that although tremendous change was happening for these families, there was little impact on the larger autistic community. I had been given an elegant and insightful system created by one autistic individual to help other autistic individuals and their families. This program changed lives. More people needed to have the opportunity to experience it.

With that goal came the birth of Davis Autism International, an organization that set out to train others in the Davis Autism Approach, in turn allowing many more autistic individuals and their families to have the opportunity to participate more fully in life. The more individuals that participated, the more evident it became that this program was the key to unlocking so many mysteries.

Unfortunately, there was still one piece missing: information. Information for those who are new to the Davis programs, information that would create an understanding of the simplicity and yet depth of this work, allow curiosities to be satisfied and informed decisions to be made. Information that would bring to light the missing element that I was searching for all those years ago.

Abigail Marshall, author of the *Everything Parent's Guide to Children with Dyslexia* and *When your child has ... Dyslexia,* has created her magic again. Together with Ron Davis, she has written this book, "Autism and the Seeds of Change." It captures the essence of our unique program, explaining it in a way that is easy to understand, and answering questions that you did not know you had.

Abigail is a gifted explainer. She can bring a third dimension to a topic allowing you to look at things from different perspectives and make solid connections. Abigail has a talent to write to a wide audience and has created a book to inform parents, grandparents, teachers and professional bodies alike. I am very grateful to have this resource, and I am sure you will be too.

Oh, and as for the young boy, eight years on, he is in high school achieving excellent grades in a broad selection of subjects and is excelling in Drama, French, English and Math. His parents do not worry for his future and enjoy watching him participate fully in life.

Lorna Timms
Director, Davis Autism International

A Note from Ron Davis

Dear Reader,

I have, for quite some time, wanted to write a manuscript with a working title of *Autism—the Gift and Curse of Real Genius*. However, my age, my changing physical condition, and my many other interests have not allowed me the time to do so.

I had hoped such a work would draw a reader's attention to a different perspective on autism. It would set the foundation for the potential for autistic individuals to gain the skills and abilities to participate fully in life. The work would have to be "lay friendly" because it would be written for the loved ones of the autistic population. But it would also need to have a bibliography to satisfy the academic community that this is a serious work, based on sound reasoning and logic, and consistent with the findings of many others.

Initially, I created a manuscript called *Nurturing the Seed of Genius*, which was the "nuts and bolts" of how to actually do this job. However, it was neither lay friendly nor academically compatible. That work was an effective workshop manual for experienced professionals, who already had the knowledge, wisdom, and understanding underlying the procedures and "tools" that are needed. But it would not meet the needs of a wider audience.

If the new book was going to happen, I needed help. Luckily, a good friend of mine would be the exactly right person to ask. Abigail Marshall is a published author in her own right. I have also worked with her in the past, co-authoring several articles, and she is thoroughly familiar with all of my work. We have been acquainted since 1995. She was among the original group that formed Davis Dyslexia Association International and she is still affiliated with that organization.

There are many that I would be willing to trust my life to, but only a few that I would be willing to trust with the future of my life's work. Abigail is one of those. In reading this book you will see that my trust isn't misplaced and just how lucky I am.

—Ron Davis

Preface:

Author's Note and Conventions

As of 2012, there are about 75 trained professionals actively working with children and adults using the Davis Autism Approach. They are working in more than a dozen countries, speaking to their clients in at least eight different languages. The Davis method occupies a distinct niche and purpose, enabling autistic individuals to bridge the gap between disability and the capacity to fully participate in life. But because the program is new, few have heard about it, and it functions below the radar of the professional and academic world.

Dozens of children and adults have completed all phases of the program, and many more are working their way through the various steps. Thus it is time for a book that will give parents and professionals a ready source of information about this revolutionary approach.

This book is not an instruction manual, and a parent, tutor or therapist should not attempt to use it as such. The best source of information for anyone who wants to work directly with an autistic individual is to seek out the coaching services of a Davis professional.[1] However, this book should provide the reader with the foundational information needed to understand the role that professionals play in guiding their autistic clients toward independence.

Davis Autism Approach Facilitator/Coaches are talented, creative, patient, skillful and highly experienced. In addition to their extensive training, they bring their own unique levels of insight and openness to their work, an element that cannot be taught or explained in a book. The "how-to" piece of the program is presently available in the form of direct coaching. Supplemental offerings such as support videos and parent workshops are in development.

In this book, I use the word "autism" broadly to refer to every manifestation of the autistic spectrum. The term includes classic autism, at any functional level; Asperger's Syndrome; Pervasive Development Disorder; and any other diagnostic label commonly considered to be on the autistic spectrum. I do so partly because current categories and labels are likely to change with the anticipated publication of the DSM V in 2013.[2]

However, I have also chosen not to use the initials ASD (for Autism Spectrum Disorder). I feel the word "disorder," encompassed within the initials, could be construed as derogatory. I do not see "autism" as a disease in need of a cure, but rather as a complex pattern of individual traits. Some of those traits are clearly quite debilitating, but others may be delightful and even awe-inspiring. Many are

---

[1] The services are available through Davis Autism International (DAI) [Web site: *www.davisautism.com*]

[2] Under the current proposal, the diagnosis of Asperger's will be abandoned and all forms of autism will be consolidated under the label "Autism Spectrum Disorder." (American Psychiatric Association 2011)

simply characteristics that have come to be woven into an individual's personality, a reflection of his own inner nature and life experience. As used in this book, the term "autism" encompasses the big picture, the good and the bad, the strengths and the weaknesses. This book is about a specific approach geared to helping autistic individuals overcome the weaknesses, without in any way diminishing or disavowing the strengths.

I sometimes use the term *autist* to refer to a person with characteristics of autism. I do that because *autist* is a noun, and a term that can equally apply to a child or adult. I do not mean to express any conclusions about the person as a whole or the nature of autism with my choice of words. I believe that each and every "autist" is a unique individual who is neither defined solely by nor demeaned by his autism.

For purposes of grammatical consistency, when referring generically to either an autistic person or a Davis client, I use the masculine pronoun, *he.* When referring generically to an adult who is working or living with autistic individuals, such as a parent, therapist or facilitator, I use the feminine, *she.* This is merely a grammatical convention adopted to avoid confusion.

This book is largely about Ronald Dell Davis, the founder of the Davis Autism Approach. I generally refer to Mr. Davis as either "Ron Davis" or "Ron" when discussing things he did or experienced as an individual and use the surname "Davis" alone primarily to refer to the methods he developed, or to his theories and ideas in relation to those methods. In other words, "Ron" is the person who invented and inspired the "Davis" methods discussed in this book.

Similarly, Davis® and Davis Autism Approach® are registered trademarks owned by Ron Davis. That means that these methods cannot be advertised or offered in a commercial context (for a fee) without licensing, and licensing can only come after extensive training and experience. Many of the specific procedures described in this book also have specific, trademarked names.

Davis professionals who have completed the rigorous training program required for licensing are designated as "Facilitator/Coaches." Facilitating is what they do when working one-on-one with an autistic client; coaching is the term used when working separately with a parent or tutor who is in turn working with an autistic client or family member. In this book I refer to such professionals generally as "facilitators"—and I use that term *only* in conjunction with licensed providers of the Davis Autism Approach Program.[3]

Finally, in the course of this book I share many anecdotes and reports conveyed by Davis Facilitators, by parents, and even directly from autistic individuals who have benefited from the Davis Autism Approach. My reference to Davis professionals includes their real, full name, but I have chosen to adopt pseudonyms for references to autists and their family members, in the interest of preserving their privacy.

—Abigail Marshall

---

[3] The function of a Davis Facilitator should not be confused with the idea of "facilitated communication," a controversial therapy for autism in which a "facilitator" provides assistance with typing to a non-verbal autistic person. Davis Facilitators are supporting an interactive learning process, with students who usually are verbal and in all cases have clear receptive language skills, with at least an ability to communicate effectively through gestures if not with words and full sentences.

Autism and the Seeds of Change

Chapter 1

The Davis Perspective on Autism

The purpose of the Davis Autism Approach is to give individuals with autistic spectrum traits the ability to participate fully in life. The program is designed to provide the core competencies, understanding, and confidence that a person needs to function independently, both in the pursuit of his own life goals, such as education and career, and in relating and integrating in society with others. That goal is achieved through a combination of self-regulatory tools for improved mental focus, together with a series of conceptual life lessons, presented in a gentle, participatory, sequential manner that promotes full mastery and integration of specific concepts.

Although the Davis approach includes techniques that can potentially help small children and other low-functioning individuals with autism, the program described in this book is not intended for early intervention. Instead, it is geared generally to older children, teenagers and adults who have good receptive language skills. The typical Davis client will be over the age of seven, and seen as moderate to high functioning.

The Davis program is not intended to "cure" autism but rather to give autistic individuals the education and tools needed to function in the world that surrounds them. The Davis program occupies a unique niche and contains some elements similar to developmental approaches to autism and social skills therapy, but with a different theoretical underpinning as well as a unique methodology.

Davis stands apart from other programs in the degree to which it is ultimately driven by the person who is pursuing the program, as opposed to the therapist or facilitator who is guiding and directing. Philosophically, Davis is a journey of self-exploration, self-discovery, self-actualization, and ultimately, self-empowerment.

The Davis program is effective because it is grounded in the autistic experience, and provides individuals with the foundational tools needed to create change within their own lives. The Davis Facilitator is planting the seeds that will enable change, but the ensuing growth is natural and nurtured by the innate capacity and inclinations of the individual.

Autism at its heart is not an impairment of cognition or intellect, but one of integration. The autist has not been able to integrate new information and experience into his life and being in the same way as non-autists or neuro-typical individuals. As the autist grows and develops, he experiences his world in a distinctly different way, which creates barriers because he does not develop a set of thoughts and behaviors that the non-autistic world takes for granted. Davis provides the autist with the missing elements, in a simple and direct way that is natural to his innate learning style. Those elements lay a path to full integration of the knowledge, wisdom, and understanding needed to navigate successfully through life.

The Roots of the Autism Program

Ronald Dell Davis developed his autism program as an extension and outgrowth of his earlier and pioneering work in the field of dyslexia. Although there is no direct relationship between autism and dyslexia, Ron Davis and his colleagues were asked to work with autistic clients even in the earliest days of the dyslexia program. As the dyslexia program was not geared toward autism, success with autistic clients was sporadic and did not fully meet their needs, but it provided a foundation of experience on which to build. The basic Davis tools are not dependent on a particular label, such as either "autism" or "dyslexia," but rather are effective ways of reaching all learners. However, to meet the unique needs of autistic clients, a new program geared specifically to autism was developed.

Ron Davis opened the Reading Research Council Dyslexia Correction Center in 1981, hiring and training counselors to assist in working with clients over the years. In 1994, after having worked with more than a thousand individuals, Ron published the first edition of his groundbreaking book, *The Gift of Dyslexia: Why Some of the Smartest People Can't Read ... and How They Can Learn.* The book was an instant success and created a groundswell of demand for the innovative Davis Dyslexia Correction Program. Partnering with other educators, Ron developed a professional training program leading to certification and licensing of hundreds of Davis Dyslexia Correction Facilitators.[4]

---

[4] A full listing of currently licensed Davis Dyslexia Correction Facilitators is available at http://www.dyslexia.com/providers.htm

The names of those qualified to provide the Davis Autism Approach can also be found at http://www.davisautism.com/contact_facilitator.html

The Davis Facilitators were confronted with many clients who were on the autistic spectrum. Some could be helped with the dyslexia-focused program; others had to be turned away. But the pool of experience to draw upon was expanded. Instead of one U.S.-based center, there were hundreds of experienced and qualified Facilitators around the world. Many were working with autistic clients on a trial basis and sharing their anecdotal reports with Ron Davis and fellow Facilitators.

By the first decade of the 21st century, a core group of highly motivated and experienced facilitators was ready to work with autistic clients, and a newly shaped program was launched and piloted. In 2008, Ron met with a dozen Facilitators for a week-long retreat in Kaikoura, New Zealand, to hammer out the specific protocols for the standardized Davis Autism Approach Program. Each of the participants had extensive experience working with Davis methods in a variety of contexts, including with autistic clients. However, the goals of a program for autism had been nebulous, with the sequence and timing of introduction of various Davis concepts left to the facilitators' individual judgment and creativity. In Kaikoura, the group established the specific sequence and protocols for the Davis Autism Approach—a new beginning, geared specifically to meet the needs of children, teenagers, and adults on the autistic spectrum.

The Davis View of Autism

Ron Davis was born in Utah in 1942, and labeled a "Kanner's Baby" in infancy. Dr. Leo Kanner first used the term "autism" to describe the syndrome he had observed in his patients in a paper published in 1943. Thus, Ron came into the world even before the word "autism" itself.

Ron clearly manifested a classic, severe form of autism. He wrote:

"My mother told me that as an infant, any physical touch from her would set me off. Even when she was trying to nurse me I would try to scream and suckle at the same time. She was so afraid that I would choke that she had to find a way of feeding me without touching me."[5]

Ron began to emerge from his autistic state in the second decade of his life. With the help of a dedicated speech therapist in his late teens, he became a functional and self-sufficient adult.

In the years since, the common understanding and diagnostic criteria of "autism" has been expanded to include other expressions of the underlying pattern, including Asperger's Syndrome and other combinations of symptoms now seen to be on the autistic spectrum.

The Davis approach is geared to addressing a specific *problem* (or set of problems) rather than a diagnosis. For purposes of the program, autism might be described as *the failure to develop behavior to the extent that the person can form and sustain social relationships.*[6]

Before a person can function effectively in relationships with others, he must first develop an understanding of *self*. He must also have the ability to make sense of his world and function capably within it. Before the autist can successfully enter social relationships, he must be on an equal footing with his peers.

---

[5] (Davis, Nurturing the Seed 2009, 5)

[6] This definition corresponds closely to Kanner's original description of autism as an "innate inability to form the usual, biologically provided affective contact with people." (Kanner, Autistic Disturbances of Affective Contact 1943, 250)

Obviously, an autist may have an array of other symptoms and problems that are not directly related to social relatedness skills. Autism also is typically accompanied by various mental strengths, which may or may not be recognized as such by those who come in contact with the autist.[7] Thus it would be inappropriate to see the Davis program as a "cure" for autism. The goal of the program is not to eliminate that which is called "autism," but rather to give the individual the capacity to develop the skills needed to participate fully in life.

Similarly, the Davis approach cannot be seen as an effort to eliminate or change undesired behaviors. Davis believes that when the reason for a behavior is eliminated, the behavior itself will cease to exist. That means that a behavior that is a compulsive response to the autist's inability to cope with his environment will recede as he gains the ability to understand and control his world. For example, autistic meltdowns are likely to disappear over time with the Davis program.

However, some autistic behaviors may remain, simply because the individual does not want or need to change those behaviors. For example, one young woman wrote after a Davis program:

> *"This program works so well, that people don't believe me anymore when I say I'm Aspergers. Not only that, I feel more free to "safely" indulge in my Aspie idiosyncrasies. I now rock back and forth and flap my hands not because I'm freaking out, but because it's fun and I like doing it! I don't have to be afraid that the dark places of my mind will*

---

[7] See, for example, (Dawson, Soulières, et al. 2007) (Dawson, Mottron and Gernsbacher, Learning in Autism 2008) (Soulières, Dawson and Samson, et al. 2009) (Mottron 2011)

take over and swallow me up just because I'm behaving Aspie. There is joy in my life and I am safe."[8]

The Davis program will provide a person with a greater level of self-awareness as well as awareness of his environment and other people in it. That will tend to make it more likely that the Davis graduate will begin to curb behaviors that seem to disturb or upset others. The young woman who posted about her "Aspie idiosyncrasies" also was able to obtain and hold down a job involving working with the public after her program, so it is likely that she had developed an understanding of an appropriate time and place for hand flapping and rocking.

But her comment illustrates a key way in which the Davis program differs from many others. There is no doubt that a person's behavior after a Davis program can and will change in significant ways, but that change will always be driven from within.

The goal of the Davis autism program is not to "fix" the individual, but rather to enable the person to function in a new way—to open a door that has previously been shut. Part of that process is to address an underlying barrier inherent in the way that the autistic brain functions; in other words, to teach the autistic person a different way to use his brain, in a conscious manner. The remainder of the process is to provide an organized and cohesive set of concepts that will provide life lessons that the person has missed because of his autistic mental state.

---

[8] Posted to a *Facebook* group, August 1, 2009. Retrieved from https://www.facebook.com/groups/6567263146/ February 26, 2012

Structure of the Davis Program

Speaking of his own autism, Ron Davis states:

> *"Way before I started working with autism or had any understanding of it, I referred to myself as having come from a void. My sense of the void was not as existing as an individual, but as existing as both nothing and everything at the same time. There was no sense of being an individual, so there was no "me". There was nothing upon which to base a sense of identity. Without a 'me,' there was no basis for memory or knowledge.*
>
> *"Somehow—by pure luck or by the grace of God— around the age of nine I began to individuate and develop out of the state of oblivion—out of the void. In hindsight, I can see there was about an eleven-year delay in my early development. Also, in hind-sight, I can see there were three phases that I had to go through to become a human being. First, I had to* **individuate***, I had to stop being everything and nothing and become just one thing, my body. Second, I had to develop an* **identity** *for the thing I had become. And third, I had to* **adapt** *to the world of being human."*[9]

The Davis Autism Approach is designed to follow the three developmental steps that Ron Davis identified in his own life: individuation, identity development, and adaptation. The third phase (adaptation) is now referred to as social integration.

The first step—*individuation*—can be either the easiest or the most difficult step of the program. It is potentially

---

[9] (Davis, Nurturing the Seed 2009, 5)

very easy because it involves the teaching of simple mental techniques that give the person control over perceptions, mental focus, mood and energy levels. It is potentially difficult because of the communication barriers that often exist with an autistic individual.

Each of the Davis mental tools is easy for a person to learn if he understands the language of the facilitator, and is receptive to her efforts. But many autistic individuals have severe impairments with language, and are wary or resistant to efforts of others to reach them. Davis professionals are given training that includes specific techniques to enhance the likelihood that an autist will accept and respond to them. Even if the autist has been resistant to overtures from other therapists or tutors who have tried to reach him in the past, there is a strong likelihood that he will accept the facilitator. For example, facilitators know to refrain from attempting to establish direct or sustained eye contact with their clients at an initial meeting, as many autists would find those actions threatening and react by withdrawing.[10]

The remaining two steps of the Davis approach are more straightforward. A person who has become individuated will be ready on a functional level to work with a facilitator, so the remainder of the program is focused on presenting a series of conceptual lessons. The lessons give the individual a framework for understanding the world he

----

[10] This is one illustration of the philosophical difference between the Davis approach and approaches such as Applied Behavior Analysis (ABA), Discrete Trial Training (DTT), or Relationship Development Intervention (RDI), which emphasize strategies to elicit and reinforce eye contact. A Davis facilitator would avoid any attempt at forcing behavior that is uncomfortable for the autist, as the goal is to seek acceptance in a manner that the prospective client would perceive as reassuring and non-threatening.

inhabits and his place within it. For the most part, these are concepts that a typically developing child would have picked up naturally through daily life, through play, and through interactions with others. But the autistic person has missed that opportunity because of his different perceptual and mental experience of his world.

The *identity development* phase typically takes the longest, as there is a long series of lessons to cover, and each must be thoroughly mastered. Through an approach called Davis Concept Mastery, the autist is guided to model a series of concepts in clay—for example, the concept of *change* or concepts such as *before* and *after*. In conjunction with modeling each concept in clay, the autist will spend time with the facilitator exploring each concept in the environment, such as looking for and discussing examples of *change, before,* and *after.* The carefully structured series of concepts starts with the simplest ideas and builds upon them to form more complex ideas. Identity development culminates with the concept of *responsibility,* because the end goal is to give the individual the ability to assume responsibility within his own life.

Of course, that doesn't mean that an autistic 12-year-old, having completed the second phase of the program, will be in a position to go out and earn a living. But the child will have progressed to the point of understanding the concept of exercising responsibility. That understanding will be exercised and developed as the child grows by allowing the child to exercise responsibility in age-appropriate areas of his own life. For example, for a child the first step is often to become responsible for keeping order in his own bedroom.

Often there is a lapse of a few weeks or months between the second and third phases of the program, in order to give the individual time to practice his newfound skills, and to experience the world with newly acquired awareness. However, the final phase does not take long, and can be completed in a day or two when the client feels ready. Like the prior phase, *social integration* relies on modeling basic concepts in clay. At this phase the concepts are specifically focused on relating self to others, and developing understanding of a set of social concepts that can be used to guide future relationships. This is not a matter of teaching social skills, such as shaking hands or making eye contact, or remembering to say "please" and "thank you." Rather the autist explores the types of relationships that can exist between or among people, such as relationships based on *trust* as contrasted with relationships based on *rules*. At the end of this stage, the person will have gained the insight and analytical schema needed to navigate life relationships and to make sound choices in forming associations and friendships.

Currently, the Davis Autism Approach is provided by licensed Davis Autism Facilitator/Coaches who either work directly with an autistic individual, or who coach a parent or other support person through the steps of working with the autist. Take-home materials for parents or support persons are included in both types of programs.

Functional Elements of Autism

Davis adopts a functional view of autism and its cause. Rather than trying to solve the mystery of its biological, medical, genetic, or neurological roots, Davis is looking at the inner world and experience of autistic individuals. What does it feel like to be inside the head of an autistic person? What is different about the autist's thoughts and feelings that prevent him from developing the life competencies that seem to come naturally for typically developing children?

Each autistic person is different. This observation is

especially true as educators and medical professionals have expanded their view over the years to include a broader range of symptom patterns under the autism umbrella. Individuals who would not have been seen as autistic 10 or 20 years ago are now widely acknowledged to fall within the autistic spectrum. More people than ever, with a wider array of behavioral and learning characteristics, are now called autistic.

But some commonalities exist that can also be seen as integral to understanding autism and providing a meaningful approach to treatment or therapy.

Autism is Developmental

The manifestations of the autistic spectrum arise during early childhood, as something the child is either born with or seems to acquire at a very young age, most commonly manifested by age three. (An older child or adult who is the victim of serious trauma or disease may display similar behaviors, but would ordinarily be diagnosed with some condition other than autism.)

Individuals with Autism Lack a Stable Orientation

"Orientation," as defined by Davis, is *the state of mind in which mental perceptions agree with the true facts and conditions in the environment.* An *oriented* person is able to focus his attention at will, to make sense of his environment, and to filter out distracting thoughts, feelings and perceptual input.

An autistic person is not able to maintain a continuous state of orientation during waking hours. The person either experiences much of life in a *disoriented* state, or else has no ability to orient at all, a state that could be described as *un-oriented.* "Disorientation" is simply the opposite of orientation; it is the state of mind when the person's mental perceptions do *not* agree with the true facts and conditions of the environment.

Individuals with Autism have Gaps in Conceptual Understanding of their World

As a direct result of the lack of stable orientation, an autistic child will experience the world differently than a typically developing child. His perceptions of sight, sound, balance, and touch will all be limited or exaggerated. Thus, the autistic child will not make the same observations, nor will he be able to draw the same inferences from experiences. Because each person is different, the conceptual gaps may be different from one individual to another. The result of these gaps and perceptual inconsistencies is that the autist experiences his world as being unpredictable, confusing and frightening.

A Solution to the Functional Limitations of Autism

With this view of autism, there is a direct, two-part solution. First, the individual needs to be provided with the ability to maintain a stable orientation, in which the person's various perceptions harmonize with each other as well as agree with the true conditions of the environment. Once the skill of establishing and maintaining orientation is acquired, the person needs to learn and explore those life concepts which are necessary to make sense of the world and his place in it. With conceptual understanding, the world is no longer seen as unpredictable and chaotic, and the person's sense of anxiety and fear dissipates.

The Davis Autism Approach is able to supply the person with both pieces: the orientation, and the concepts. Doing so fills the developmental gap, ultimately enabling the autistic person to function capably and independently, and to meaningfully participate in life.

Whether or not the person is still autistic depends on how one sees and defines "autism." If you look at autism through the lens of its most disabling aspects, then the Davis program will eliminate the cause of those disabilities, and to that extent the autism has been corrected. However, nothing in the Davis program would detract in any way from gifts and talents that the person may have, nor from the unique perspective he may have gained as part of his autistic experience. The autistic child who was fascinated with trains and train schedules may continue to nurture that fascination. Or perhaps he will move on and develop a broader set of interests. The Davis program opens a new door on life, but does not shut the door on the past nor detract from the spirit of the individual.

Chapter 2

How the Davis Tools Were Developed

Although it is a new program, the Davis Autism Approach is based on more than a quarter century of practical, hands-on experience working with individuals with autism as well as a variety of other learning or behavioral difficulties. Ron Davis' own personal history with autism did not endow him with any special ability when it comes to helping others, but it did give him the insight that comes from a shared experience. He also had the benefit of hindsight, enabling him to structure an approach based on the steps that he himself had to complete to become a competent and independent adult.

Ron Davis' Childhood and Youth

Ron Davis has only the vaguest of memories of the first decade of his life. He usually describes his early childhood experience as being *"in the void,"* as existing as *"both nothing and everything at the same time."*

But Ron does know that his first steps to emerging from that void involved building a conceptual representation of his world in clay. He writes,

15

"Somewhere in the void of autism, I discovered that by mixing dirt and water together in a puddle, in the back yard, I could make a thick goo. This substance could be formed into anything I wanted. The dirt in our back yard was a gummy red clay. If you let it dry completely, it would hold its shape for a long time."[11]

At first he used the clay dirt to form objects he coveted. His brothers were allowed to have pocket-knives and watches. The only time he had gotten hold of a real pocket-knife, he had nearly cut off a finger. With no concept of time he had no clue as to what a wristwatch was good for. But those were objects forbidden to him that his brothers owned and used, and so he wanted them. He made himself a clay dirt pocket-knife, and then another; and he made himself watches from clay dirt and string. He'd keep each new pocket-knife in his pocket until it crumbled, and his watch tied to his wrist until it broke, and then he'd fashion another.

At age 12, Ron was labeled with "uneducable mental retardation" and the school abandoned efforts to teach him. But somehow his curiosity was aroused about the alphabet letters displayed on a banner on his classroom wall, and he began to make models of clay dirt letters on his own. Eventually he had fashioned and memorized each letter of the alphabet and its name. When asked to recite the alphabet, he could name all 26 letters, but they would be in the random order he had made them. Later on, he set about learning the proper sequence of the letters when arrayed in alphabetical order.

At age 17, Ron was tested again. Surprisingly, his IQ score had risen to 137, clearly in the gifted range. At that

---

[11] (Davis, Red Dirt and Water 1997)

point he began to work with a speech and language therapist, Dr. Meredith Evans, and he was given tutoring to
help him learn to read. The speech therapy worked. The
reading instruction didn't, and Ron was told that he would
probably never learn to read or write due to brain damage
suffered at birth.

Ron writes,

*"When I learned to speak, words became part of
my universe, so when I made a model of an idea, I
also began to make the name of the idea. Between
the ages of 17 and 27, I created more than a thousand ideas and words in modeling clay. By the
time I was 27, my IQ score had risen to 169."*[12]

Though Ron couldn't read, he had a knack for mathematics, associated with exceptional visual-spatial skills. As
a child Ron manifested savant-like qualities, able to give
correct answers to complex trigonometry problems even
though he didn't have the slightest clue as to how he
arrived at the answer; a visual representation of the
answer would simply pop into his head when he heard the
question. His mother was terrified at the idea of her son
being labeled as some sort of freak of nature, however, and

---

[12] (Davis, Red Dirt and Water 1997) The rising IQ scores may
be a reflection of the inadequacy of the then-available instruments
used to measure IQ, as well as Ron Davis' emerging intellect
through his adolescence and young adulthood. Current research
shows that both children and adults with autism and Asperger's,
scored significantly higher when IQ is assessed using the nonverbal
Raven's Advanced Progressive Matrices, as compared to the
Weschler scales. The discrepancy—an average 30 percentile points
for the autistic group—meant that many children determined to
have below-average intelligence with traditional tests had measur-
able intelligence significantly above average when tested using the
Ravens instrument. (Dawson, Soulières, et al. 2007) (Soulières,
Dawson and Gernsbacher, et al. 2011)

discouraged efforts to recognize or develop that talent.[13]

The savant-type skills did not survive Ron's acquisition of language, but his basic affinity for math did persist, opening the door to a technically-oriented career. In the 1960's, at the height of the Cold War and the space race, the aerospace industry was eager to hire and train qualified technicians, and Ron did well with the hands-on training they offered. He excelled at making precision measurements, as well as being involved in new uses of optical equipment and converting electronic anomalies to physical dimension measurements. Eventually he gained a position as a certified engineer focusing on non-destructive testing in the guided missile industry. Thus he had gainful employment for many years, until ultimately he was promoted to levels where the ability to read and write technical reports became more important. Eventually there was no way to keep up with the written demands of his job, or to continue to fake his way through the situations requiring literacy, and Ron shifted to other pursuits.

A Solution to Dyslexia

In 1980, at age 38, Ron Davis had a sudden insight as to his own dyslexia. His hunch led to a discovery that ultimately allowed him to help thousands of children and adults with a wide variety of learning barriers, and also provided an entry to working with autistic clients.

---

[13] During Ron's childhood, the term "savant" would have been coupled with the term "idiot." Unfortunately, throughout most of the latter half of the twentieth century, it was common practice for educators and therapists to attempt to suppress rather than encourage unusual talents seen in autistic youngsters, as it was assumed that the development of such abilities reflected a mental pathology and played a part in preventing normal development. See (Dawson, Mottron and Gernsbacher, Learning in Autism 2008)

Ron knew that the symptoms of his dyslexia varied at different times, and observed a correlation while working in his new vocation as a sculptor. While sculpting, he noticed that when he was at his artistic best, he was at his dyslexic worst.

As an engineer, he reasoned that if the dyslexia could be made worse, then there must be a way to make it better. Obviously there was something he was doing with his mind when sculpting that made the dyslexia worse, so he began to self-monitor his thought processes while sculpting. He realized that he habitually shifted his mental perspective so that he could visualize his work from many angles. He wondered whether his shifting of his "mind's eye" was at the root of his dyslexia.

Like most dyslexic adults, Ron had rudimentary reading skills—he knew how letters could be put together to form words, but it was painstaking and difficult for him to decipher the words. For Ron, the words seemed to shimmer and bounce on the page, shrinking and jumbling together with each successive line of text. If he could shift his perspective to make his dyslexia worse, he wondered if there was an alternate type of shifting he could do that would improve his ability to focus on the text and read.

To satisfy his curiosity, Ron rented a private motel room so that he could experiment with shifting his mental focus without distractions. He imagined that he was moving his mind's eye in, out, up, down, and around himself, his head, his body, and the room. From each different position he would try to focus and read some printed object, hoping to eventually find a spot that was less confusing than the others.

Ron's experiments made him feel dizzy and nauseous. He gave himself a headache. He made himself physically ill. But after three days of mental meandering, he discovered a place where the letters and words no longer moved, shrunk or ran together. The key was to park his mind's eye at a point outside his body, centered along his midline, above and slightly to the rear of his head. He picked up an informational card in the hotel and marveled that the letters stood still. They were the same size, spaced evenly apart with wider spaces between each word at the top of the card, and at the bottom. Every word stood still and the letters were sharply defined. Ron then walked to a nearby public library to find a real book. He picked up the book *Treasure Island*, and read it cover to cover in one sitting. And he understood what the words meant.

That was the first time Ron had finished reading a book in his life. And the very first time, ever, that he had enjoyed reading. But, more importantly for him, it was a milestone in the fulfillment of his lifelong dream—to become a "real human being."

Although he did not know it at the time, Ron's discovery that shifting his mental perspective had an impact on the way he perceived and interpreted print would also provide a bridge into the world of autism. At the time, Ron knew merely that he had found a way to overcome his last remaining barrier, by gaining the ability to decipher meaning from print.

Ron was ecstatic. He returned home and told his family and friends that he had found a cure for his dyslexia. At first he thought that "cure" meant that he hadn't really been dyslexic after all, that there was just some strange oddity about his own mind, and that he had simply hit upon the way to set himself straight. As Ron shared his story with friends, many of them also confessed to having dyslexia or a lifelong reading problem. They insisted that he demonstrate his dyslexia-fixing strategy, and he took each friend through the same process, guiding them to shift their mental perspective around until they found the spot where the letters stood still. And in every case, it worked.

Ron assigned the name "orientation point" to the mental spot that seemed to optimize perceptions for reading. He rented office space and set up a clinic to study the process of orientation and reading. Over time, he became more efficient at guiding others to find their orientation point, eventually writing a scripted approach that is now known as Davis Orientation Counseling.[14] By 1982, Ron was confident that he knew enough about dyslexia to hire support staff and offer dyslexia correction services to the public. Soon he and his employees would discover that the orientation counseling tool, with its impact on perception, offered benefits that extended far beyond the realm of dyslexia.

Orientation and Perception

Ron Davis had discovered that his own mental orientation was tied closely to perception. When he brought his mind's eye to his orientation point, his perceptions were accurate; when off point, perceptions were often distorted and mistaken. He also had discovered through his work that other dyslexic adults shared the same experience.

However, Ron's theory was viewed with skepticism and even ridicule by educators and academic experts who were entrenched in their view that dyslexia was tied to a specific brain defect. Ron wanted to prove his hypothesis that the perceptual confusion associated with dyslexia was tied to disorientation, so he designed his own experiment.

---

[14] Full instructions for the Davis Orientation Counseling procedure are contained in Ron Davis' book, *The Gift of Dyslexia.* (Davis and Braun, Gift of Dyslexia 2010)

To create a sense of disorientation, Ron affixed a large cardboard disk with a painted spiral onto a turntable, using a foot switch to control the spinning of the disk. He then became his own first test subject, armed with a stopwatch, tape recorder, and clipboard.[15]

Ron sat in front of the turntable and stared into the center of the spiral. He pressed his foot and the disk began to spin. In less than five seconds he felt a sense of motion, as if he were flying down an endless tunnel. Ron stopped and started again. When he repeated the experiment, he noticed that the spinning disk appeared to slow down just before he had the sensation of movement. So in addition to a distorted perception of motion, Ron experienced an change in his sense of vision.

Ron tried to stand in front of the disk balancing on one foot. He fell over backward. Clearly, the spinning disk affected his sense of balance.

He sat in front of the disk with his stopwatch. While the disk was still, he looked at the center and estimated the passage of 15 seconds, by clicking the stopwatch on and off without looking at it. He repeated the exercise five times, and was never any more than three seconds off. Then he set the disk spinning and tried again, also with five trials. When the disk was spinning, he never managed to get any closer than five seconds with his guesses and twice was more than ten seconds off. The sense of time was definitely distorted.

Then Ron turned on his tape recorder. After he felt the sense of motion, he signaled to an assistant. His helper was instructed to say something to him, so that he would repeat back what he had heard. They used familiar nursery rhymes or tongue twisters, but the assistant was

---

[15]   (Davis, My Study of Disorientation 1997).

instructed to deliberately alter the words so that they could not be recited from memory. Ron discovered that, disoriented, he could not hear the exact words spoken. The proof was on the tape.

Ron decided to recruit 100 adult volunteers to participate in an experiment in a makeshift lab, where he would measure their ability to perceive accurately, on each of the tests he had created. It didn't matter for purposes of the experiment whether the test subjects were dyslexic or not. He knew from experience that just about anybody occasionally felt disoriented. The point of the experiment was simply to test the hypothesis that disorientation caused altered perceptions.

Ron began to do his experiment with anyone willing to sit in front of the spinning disk. He asked his volunteers to let him know when they first felt a sense of movement, and then proceeded with each of the tests in turn. Some people were made too nauseous by the spinning disk to complete all four phases of the trial, but all experienced sensory distortions in the phases that they did complete. Among those who were able to complete the full series, everyone experienced distortion in all the senses measured: vision, hearing, balance, motion, and time.

Unfortunately, Ron ultimately learned that his experiment was quite dangerous. Occasionally a person would sit in front of the spinning disk for up to five minutes and not feel the sensation of flying through the endless tunnel.

The subject would get nauseous, but would not experience any sense of movement.

Ron's 48th volunteer was a young woman who reported feeling no sense of movement for three full minutes staring at the spinning disk. Then she fell to the floor with a *gran mal* epileptic seizure. Ron was terrified, and rightfully so— the event was unexpected as the woman had never suffered a seizure before.

So Ron ended the experiment, satisfied that he had confirmed his hypothesis about the relationship between disorientation, perceptions and dyslexia. He also had an inkling as to a possible reason for the altered perceptions: perhaps it is the brain's way of avoiding overload in confusing circumstances, a much safer response than the seizure he had seen in the young woman whose perceptions had seemed to hold steady.

Ron's demonstration of the connection between orientation, disorientation, and the accuracy of perceptions also provides insight into the sensory confusion that is a common part of the autistic experience.

Different Roads to Orientation

When Ron opened his California center for dyslexia correction in 1982, he knew of one path to orientation. He guided his clients through a visualization exercise based on the same mind's eye shifting he had managed for himself. He also discovered over time that each person shared the same approximate spot to orient for reading. He then developed a short, scripted approach to guide each client. The initial orientation session could be completed in about 20 minutes, with a second session to refine the skill after a few days of practice.

The majority of dyslexics who sought help at the center could easily experience their mind's eye moving about. At first Ron assumed that all dyslexics shared the gift of picture-based thinking and the ability to easily shift their perspective while visualizing imagined objects. However, about a year after the center had opened, Ron hired an assistant named Albert who insisted that he was dyslexic, but was not able to follow the orientation procedure. Albert, and others like him, would need another approach.

Since the key seemed to be some sort of stabilizing force above and behind the head, Ron wondered if there was a way to achieve a similar result through tactile imagination rather than visualization. Ron worked with Albert until together they hit upon the idea of imagining a pair of steadying hands resting on Albert's shoulders.

That method is now called Davis Alignment.[16] The overall effect is slightly different than the mind's eye orientation, but the practical result is the same. Perceptions are stabilized, the person feels balanced and centered, and experiences a sense of calm and relaxed focus. Instead of visualizing a mental point, the person regains their alignment when needed by remembering the feeling of the hands on his shoulders.

With Alignment, the Davis center could provide all of its clients with the tools needed to orient themselves at will. Among the highly functional adults and children who came to the center for help with dyslexia or related learning difficulties, all could easily learn one technique or another.

But that still left the problem of how to reach autistic clients.

---

[16] The Davis Alignment procedure is described, along with full instructions, in *The Gift of Dyslexia*. (Davis and Braun, Gift of Dyslexia 2010)

Ron had not set out to try to correct autism, but he couldn't easily forget his own past. Whether he sought them or not, parents of autistic children would arrive, hoping for some sort of relief. Ron and his staff could often help the higher functioning autists who arrived seeking help for reading problems or other academic issues. If a person was able and willing to listen to and follow a facilitator's instruction, then orientation or alignment could always be achieved. And it made a world of difference, especially for children who seemed to be frequently unfocused or lost in their own thoughts.

However, some parents brought autistic children who were nonverbal, perhaps motivated by anecdotal reports of Ron's success with some of the higher functioning children. But those children didn't speak, and it was also not clear what, if any, spoken words they understood. Ron needed to find a way to reach them that didn't involve talking to them or explaining what to do. He needed some sort of system of automatic, self-orientation.

Ron wondered if the key to reaching the autistic mind was through hearing.

In 1983, Ron did an experiment with a 9-year-old autistic boy named Kevin. Kevin was a tiny kid, unusually small for his age, and he had no speech. Ron could tell from the doorway that the boy was one of the more severely autistic children he'd seen. His face looked unwashed, his hair uncut, unwashed, and uncombed. He even had streaks below his nose. When his mother pushed him into Ron's office he quickly disappeared behind the drapery. Ron asked if the boy spoke and his mom said, "Not a single word, he makes noises but not words." Ron asked if he could do a little experiment, by putting a head set on the boy to see how he would react. His mother's reaction was a simple caution, "He bites."

Ron lured Kevin out from behind the drapery and

managed to get the headset on him without any trouble. The headset was attached to a Sony Walkman that was tuned into a local radio station. The boy's reaction was remarkable—he seemed to be frozen by the sound. The Walkman was tuned to an AM, monaural station—so the sound that came through the stereo headset was the same for each ear. Ron knew that, wearing the headsets, it would seem to Kevin as if the sound was coming from inside his head, in the center. This wasn't quite where an orientation point needed to be, but it was a start.

Ron's simple experiment quickly grew into an agreement with the mother to allow Kevin to wear the headset as much as he wanted to every day. It turned out that he wanted it about eight hours a day.

Almost exactly two months later Kevin's mom called, extremely excited, saying "Kevin said his first words today!" Curious, Ron asked, "What did he say?" The mom replied, "Oh what a feeling, Toyota!"

Obviously Kevin still had a way to go, but a barrier had been broken. A few months later, Kevin's mother called again, delighted to report that her son had moved beyond echoing speech and was using personal pronouns— *you/me/I*—correctly in sentences.

Ron's next step was to construct a device that would enable a person to hear a consistent sound, emanating from the ideal point for orientation. That meant a sound that came from above and behind the head.

Ron designed a microphone to record the sound of a titanium chime with a reverberating tone in a way that would precisely replicate the spatial location of the tone. The recorded tone was repeated at regular intervals. A person who is oriented while listening will accurately hear the tone as being localized at the orientation point, centered slightly above and behind the head. Because of the repetition and reverberation, a person who is not oriented while listening will eventually become oriented, as their attention is naturally brought back again and again to the source of the sound. Ron's device was the first step to giving autistic clients the tool of orientation, but that was only a beginning. Orientation training eliminates a barrier; it does not solve the problems that have developed over time as a result of the barrier.

Fixing the Problem

When prospective clients come to Ron Davis' center, the first step is to define the problem they need help with. Since Ron was initially offering a program for "dyslexia correction," most of his clients had trouble with reading or writing. But sometimes clients with the label "dyslexia" turned out to have other needs, such as difficulty with math. There is a high correlation between dyslexia and ADHD (attention deficit disorder), so many Davis clients also needed help with issues such as organizational skills and impulse control.

All clients began with the orientation tools, using mind's eye orientation, alignment, or auditory orientation, depending upon their individual learning style and needs. But orientation training merely sets the stage, by ensuring that the person is ready to learn—that attention can be focused on the task at hand, and that perceptions are accurate. The main part of a Davis program is providing a specific means for the person to become proficient in the skills they were unable to acquire prior to coming in for the program.

Ron understood that the main reason his dyslexic clients got disoriented in the first place was as a reaction to confusion or frustration. In fact, disorientation is a very normal reaction to strong feelings of confusion.[17] But people who are labeled as having learning disabilities seem to have a very low tolerance for confusion, and hence become disoriented more frequently. Ron realized that the way to avoid disorientation was to find and eliminate whatever factors triggered feelings of confusion or frustration. For children and adults who had problems with reading, that process began with learning the letters of the alphabet.

As Ron had spent much of his childhood and early adult life modeling words in clay in order to understand them, it was natural for him to use clay as the primary instrument of learning for his clients. Clay also had the advantage of being readily available and adaptable to different circumstances. Ron also believes that the creative process is indispensible to learning; certainly most dyslexics seem to learn best with hands-on approaches.

For a dyslexia program, the additional steps were geared to building the ability to understand letters and words. First the client would model all of the letters of the alphabet, upper and lower case. Then, when it was determined that all of the letters were truly mastered—that is, that none triggered disorientation—the client moved on to modeling words in clay, by creating both a representation of the meaning of the word and spelling out the letters of the word. That process is called Davis Symbol Mastery.

The clay modeling approach is grounded on Ron's

---

[17] Psychologists Jerome Bruner and Leo Bruner established the impact of stress and frustration on perception through research carried out in the 1940's. Subjects experienced "perceptual disruption" and deterioration of perceptual responses when asked to make rapid judgments under confusing or stressful conditions. (Postman and Bruner 1948) (Bruner and Postman 1949)

insight that dyslexics are generally nonverbal thinkers. Most think primarily in pictures, and experience confusion when they don't have a mental picture to go along with words encountered in print.[18] The words that cause the most trouble end up being the small, function words of language—words like *and, the, for, then.* Because those are also the words most frequently encountered in print, mastery of those words goes a long way to building reading fluency. Because those words are triggers for disorient-tation, Ron called them "trigger" words and developed a list of 217 English words for his dyslexic clients to master.

For other learning and behavioral problems, Ron devel-oped additional strategies. Clay still remained a primary tool, since it could be used for just about every type of learning. For mathematics, Ron developed a series of exer-cises using clay to represent numeric concepts, such as constructing a grid of clay balls and clay ropes to represent the process of multiplication. A client needing help with math could also model the meanings of math words in clay—words like *from, into, and,* or *by* have somewhat different meanings when they are encountered in the context of a math problem, and concepts such as *division* or *fraction* can also be represented in clay.

When a client came in seeking help for attention deficit disorder (ADHD), the solution became more complex. Typically, children would have a variety of behavioral problems and adult clients would have issues related to organizational skills, such as difficulty meeting deadlines or completing projects. Though others might attribute these problems merely to inattention, Ron recognized that his clients needed to gain an understanding of basic

---

[18] Recent research suggests that roughly 85% of dyslexic adults manifest a preference for visual rather than verbal problem-solving strategies. (Bacon and Handley 2010)

concepts integral to various life skills. For example, a client who was disorderly needed to explore the concepts of *order* and *disorder,* and to properly understand *order,* the person also needed to understand *time* and *sequence.* Those concepts were often missing because of the attention focus problems that had given rise to the ADHD diagnosis.

Ron applied clay to a process for learning these ideas, dubbing his method Davis Concept Mastery. Rather than being focused on learning words simply to be able to read them, Concept Mastery is geared to mastering the ideas the words represent, and the relationships between simple and more complex ideas. The tools of Concept Mastery could be given to clients on an as-needed basis, depending on specific problem areas, or via an entirely separate and more complete Davis Attention Mastery program.

In essence, Concept Mastery is a clay modeling program developed to help a person build life and relationship skills. Those are exactly the same skills that are needed to help a person with autism. The only difference is that the autistic person is likely to need a lot more help and guidance than the so-called "neurotypical" person who merely carries the label ADHD. The autistic individual also needs a more complete and more structured program, one that is designed so that there is no possibility of unfilled gaps or missed pieces.

Creating a Program for Autism

The creation of a Davis program specifically to address autism did not require new techniques. But it did require a new structure and changes in the method of delivery.

When Ron Davis' book *The Gift of Dyslexia* was published in 1994, it set the stage for a formal program of training and licensing Davis providers. Because the book was translated into many languages, there was a demand for qualified professionals in many parts of the world. By 1996, a full program of training had been created, and by the turn of the century, there were hundreds of licensed Davis Facilitators working with children and adults all over the world.

Many facilitators worked with autistic clients on an *ad hoc* basis. That is, they used the knowledge gained from their training and work with other clients and tried to give autistic clients the same tools, in whatever time frame and whatever order seemed to work for those individuals. Of course, they did this work with mixed results. In general, their clients experienced some improvement, but as there was no clear end point nor uniform set of goals for an autism program, it was hard for facilitators to know where to leave off.

Ron began to work with a core group of facilitators to create a more structured program. A rough outline of the program, of all concepts to be covered and the order they would be presented, was drawn up. One facilitator, Lorna Timms of New Zealand, had worked with a high functioning autistic boy who could not complete the dyslexia program. He seemed like an ideal candidate for an autism program. He was bright and engaging but he had an array of behavioral quirks and social deficits that made it clear to anyone who met him that he was quite autistic. So he became the first child to go through a formal Davis Autism program. I'll call him Max.

In 2008, Ron met with Lorna Timms and 10 other facilitators in Kaikoura, New Zealand. All were highly experienced Davis providers, some were Davis Specialists or Trainers, and many already had a great deal of experience working with autistic clients, even without a formal program.[19] Max's parents also came to lend their perspective in group discussions. Max was there as well, but could spend most of his time playing and exploring the farm where the retreat was held.

The Kaikoura group worked together to hammer out the details of the final autism program. Lorna shared her experiences with Max—he had completed every single step that Lorna, with Ron's input, had laid before him. At that meeting, they came to a consensus as to the specific steps of an autism program, and agreed on the specific vocabulary to be used.

The end result was a complete and very highly structured program. Every concept that needs to be mastered is part of the program, but each and every concept is presented in a direct and simple way. Each new concept builds on something already presented, and there are no extraneous or unnecessary ideas or concepts.

A person who successfully completes the Davis Autism Program will emerge at the end with the ability to participate fully in life—with the knowledge, understanding, and wisdom he needs to make sense of the world around him and of his place within that world. He will be able to make plans and set goals for himself, to work toward those goals, and to interact and form relationships with other people in his world.

Ron wrote a training manual for autism facilitators and titled it *Nurturing the Seed of Genius.* He chose that title because he truly believes that each and every autistic person has an innate potential to develop an extraordinary

---

[19] Davis Specialists, Trainers and Workshop Presenters are highly experienced facilitators who are qualified to fill specific roles in training new facilitators, or training current facilitators for more specialized roles.

level of intelligence. The problem that is manifested as *autism* is not a defect or a lack of brain power, but rather that the person is overwhelmed by more brain power than he can manage in the chaos of un-orientation. The Davis approach solves both the chaos and the management problems, thus providing each client with the ability to fully develop his intellect and life potential.

Chapter 3

Orientation and Individuation

"Spinning my body
Brings some sort of harmony to my thoughts...
The trouble is when I stop spinning
My body scatters..."

Tito Rajarshi Mukhodopadhyay[20]

The first phase of the Davis Autism Approach is *Individuation*. During this phase the autistic person will be given appropriate tools to achieve a state of orientation. The client will also be given other mental and emotional self-regulation techniques, if he is ready to learn them. Typically this phase would begin with the facilitator

---

[20] Tito Rajarshi Mukhopadhyay is a severely autistic young man who grew up in Bangalore, India. Through his mother's intense efforts, he learned to communicate through independent writing, even though he could not speak. This poem comes from the book *The Mind Tree* (Mukhopadhyay 2003, poem 4, p. 204), which contains texts Tito produced between ages 8 and 11. (Reprinted by permission of Arcade Publishing, Inc.)

meeting the autist and establishing the rapport needed to go forward. In some cases, especially with younger children or with individuals with severe autism, the individual will not be ready. In those cases, the facilitator may give the parent a recording of the auditory orientation sequence for the child to listen to at home. Over time, merely listening to the tone can bring about a sufficient degree of change to allow a facilitator to start working with the child.

The Importance of Being Oriented

An infant is born with 100 billion neurons in his brain. Each brain cell has a thousand to ten thousand synapses, branching out and forming trillions of separate connections with other brain cells.[21] In the month before birth, almost 40,000 new synapses are formed each second; after birth, the growth of neural connections accelerates exponentially through the first year of life.[22] By the time the baby is a year old, his brain will have a thousand trillion synapses connecting each neuron with thousands of others. But even as the synaptic density continues to increase, the normally developing baby is beginning to shed excess connections in a process called pruning.

At birth, most of the connections needed for sensory function are already in place—the brain is ready for the child to hear, see, taste, smell, and feel. But the newborn infant lives in a world of fleeting and disorganized sensations. In order to make sense of the world, the infant brain must begin to recognize patterns from all the sensory stimuli. He must learn to organize the sensory input

---

[21] Recent research suggests that infants who later develop autism have 67% *more* brain cells in their prefrontal cortex than typically developing babies. (Courchesne, et al. 2011)

[22] (Tau and Peterson 2010)

so that his eyes can match color and shape and texture together to recognize a pale blue blanket, a yellow rattle, his mother's long brown hair. He must learn to use his hearing to determine the direction of a sound, to put together timbre and pitch so that he can recognize his mother's voice, to learn to respond to the rhythms and melodies of a familiar lullaby, to learn to separate the sounds of birds chirping outside his window from the sound of a whirring fan in his bedroom. And he must begin to learn to coordinate his body movements, to reach for a toy, to grasp, to hold his head steady, to sit up on his own without falling over, to pull himself up to a standing position.

All of this is accompanied by the brain pruning process. Over time, some brain connections are strengthened, and those that are not used are discarded. Instead of a massive jumble of connections, the brain creates a system of internal, functional connections that enable the growing baby to learn to play and walk and talk, to focus his attention at will, to filter out unneeded and distracting information, and to develop a conscious awareness of his own body as separate and apart from his environment.

But for the autistic child, it doesn't come together.[23] The brain does not develop the capacity to harmonize input, to make sense of the external world, or gain those skills of attention focus and filtering out distractions. The child may be hypersensitive to stimuli and overwhelmed. It is likely that the autistic child was born with substantially

---

[23] Though Davis uses his own terminology to describe the brain states of orientation and disorientation, many researchers agree that autism is characterized by difficulties with neural synchronization. For example, one research team found that 70% of autistic toddlers showed disrupted synchronization across the two brain hemispheres, even during sleep. (Dinstein, et al. 2011)

more neurons in frontal areas of his brain, and the brains of many autistic children continue to grow at an accelerated rate until age two.[24] But the pathways that connect the brain cells do not keep up.[25] An overabundance of brain cells at an early age, coupled with less efficient development of connective pathways, may explain why an autistic child can have too much going on at once in his head to cope. It can also explain why some children seem to be progressing normally, and then regress and withdraw in the second or third year of life; they may simply reach a point where the mismatch between brain neuron development and connective fiber development becomes overwhelming.

The Concept of Orientation

Orientation is simply the term that Davis uses to describe the mental state that goes along with being able to focus attention, perceive the world accurately, and filter out distracting stimuli. Davis defines orientation as follows:

---

[24] The atypically high rate of brain growth has been documented only in boys, and may relate only to one subtype of autism. Autistic girls seem to follow a different pattern and also are likely to display symptoms of autism earlier. The period of excess growth seen in many boys is followed by a period of much slower growth in later childhood; by adulthood their brain size will be about the same as typically developing individuals. (Courchesne, et al. 2011) (Redcay and Courchesne 2005)

[25] A recent study shows that age 6 months, infants who later develop autism have significantly elevated levels of white matter fiber tract development. But the rate of growth is much slower than infants who do not develop autism, and by age 24 months brain scans show comparatively reduced evidence of fiber tract development. (Wolff, et al. 2012)

Orientation: A state of mind in which mental perceptions agree with the true facts and conditions in the environment.

A typically developing child will probably begin to develop the ability to orient himself during the first year of life. That capacity becomes apparent as the baby begins to engage in purposeful play or other activities—not merely to grab or wave a rattle, but to examine an object in his hand, or deliberately pick up a morsel of food. At first the periods of orientation will be very brief. As the child grows, he will spend more time during his day in an oriented state, with longer duration of periods of orientation. His parents might see these periods as evidence of a developing attention span as they observe the child's play, and he becomes more responsive to communication from older children and adults.

With the ability to orient, a foundation is laid for the development of speech—the child will be able to hear and make sense of the sound patterns of the language spoken around him, eventually to form words on his own.

No one is oriented all the time, and a small child's periods of orientation are probably very fleeting at first. But with the ability to orient, the child will begin to discern patterns in the world, and be able to make sense of what happens around him. Orientation allows him to develop a sense of the passage of time, which in turn will allow him to observe and recognize patterns of cause and effect. Orientation allows him to develop a sense of his position in space, to judge where he is in relation to objects around him. It allows him to hear sounds in his environment accurately and consistently, so that he will be able to discern words that are spoken to him, and to sort out one voice from another. Over time, orientation will allow the child to develop a sense of normalcy, to recognize continuity in his environment, and to feel secure and confident in familiar surroundings.

The child will also begin to develop the ability to distinguish between orientation and disorientation. A child engaged in imaginative play is often in a state of disorientation; rather than being aware of the true state of his environment, he has chosen to enter an imaginary world, one in which his toy truck is perceived as real, his stuffed animals can talk, and he may very well have an imaginary friend, seen by him but invisible to others. But the typically developing child is applying many of the rules from his real-world environment to his imaginary world, and often using the imaginary world to role-play real world situations. He may sometimes be confused as to what is real and imaginary, but his brain is engaged in the process of sorting all of that out.

If a child does not develop the ability to orient himself, he will inhabit a world of chaos or confusion. He won't be able to make sense of words that are spoken to him, or learn his mother tongue. He will have difficulty discerning the ordinary from the unusual, unable to recognize a myriad of patterns of activities and events in his world. He won't be able to *disorient* with imaginary play, because he won't have developed any sense of what the real world is, so no internal structure on which to base a pretend world.

Many of the typical behaviors of classic autism can be understood in light of this internal, chaotic world. If the child cannot make sense of his surroundings, the world becomes a fearful and unpredictable place. So the autistic child may engage in repetitive behaviors because those are the only constants in his life. A fascination with spinning objects may reflect a drive to somehow achieve a faux sense of orientation through the consistent, circulating motion of the object. Alternatively it might be a symptom of an inability to maintain a sense of orientation separate and apart from the spinning object.

A compulsion to arrange toys on a shelf in a rigid, unvarying array may be that child's effort to create some sense of consistency in an inconstant world. The child may panic at the slightest variation in routine because, without orientation, he has not developed the ability to weigh and compare similar events in his life, to intuit a set of rules in some situations and know when to apply them in others. He retreats into his own world because he does not have the capacity to cope or engage with the people around him.

Variations in Developmental Patterns

The pattern of development may vary, as does the level of function, but the root cause is the brain's inability to properly reconcile and interpret perceptual input. The disruption is not so global as to preclude all learning; many autistic children acquire basic motor function (such as the ability to crawl, walk, or use their hands to grasp and manipulate objects) around the same time as typically developing children. But the brain's motor cortex governs more primitive functions, probably driven by an innate biological imperative and strong, instinctual urges. The issues confronted in autism, as well as with learning difficulties such as dyslexia and ADHD, arise because of developmental lapses or differences related to more complex cognitive functioning. The degree of impairment and specific areas of function may vary, but the common characteristic is that the brain is not making the connections that are needed to achieve optimum function as a human being within present-day society.

Specific difficulties may be tied to specific brain areas. For example, the frontal cortex is implicated in higher level rational thought, executive function, and inhibition of emotionally driven behavior. The anterior cingulate cortex is particularly important in the interpretation of signals from various parts of the brain, such as coordinating signals from the emotional, limbic system (which include the amygdala and hippocampus) with signals from the frontal lobe, and in recognizing and reconciling conflicting or unexpected stimuli. Left hemispheric regions are important to the development of language and linear, sequential patterns of thought. If some parts of the autistic brain are active and highly functional, but not forming efficient connections to other parts of the brain, then the path of development will be shifted in favor of the parts that work well.

Orientation is simply a state of mind which is a necessary precursor to development of some of the more complex types of brain function, such as language facility and abstract thought. If the person *feels* confused, that mental feeling arises because his brain is somehow not able to process or reconcile sensory information at the time the person registers the feeling of confusion. As long as the person is in a state of confusion, he will be unable to learn from the experience that has given rise to the confusion, except perhaps to acquire an emotional reaction that leads him to avoid whatever it is that makes him feel uncomfortable. "Learning" is the behavioral manifestation of the brain's process of self-wiring; when a person learns something new, somewhere inside his head the brain has strengthened the connections needed to express that knowledge or ability.

All people feel confused some of the time—and the sense of confusion is always associated with disorientation. That is, one definition of *disorientation* might be *the state of feeling confused.* But for typically-developing individuals, periods of confusion are temporary and short-lived, replaced by understanding and a sense of competence. Of course, some situations are likely to be confusing or overwhelming for anyone. What differentiates an autistic person or someone labeled as having a learning disability is persistent confusion in areas of function that seem to be easily acquired and managed by others.

To a certain extent, the sense that the person is "disabled" or impaired in some way is imposed by societal norms rather than innate biology. Human society as a whole has come to expect that growing children will easily acquire the types of knowledge and behavior patterns that seem easy for most of the people in that society to learn and acquire. At the same time, society places little importance on the acquisition of knowledge and behavior patterns that are difficult or elusive for most to acquire. Thus, an autist who has developed exceptional prowess in areas as diverse as music, art, or mathematics may be labeled a *savant*, but still seen as severely impaired because of awkward social skills, such as the inability to engage in small talk at parties. Yet no child or adult who *lacks* competence in music or art or is unable to understand advanced mathematical concepts is seen as having a disability or brain-based disorder.[26]

It may well be that many autists would do just fine, without intervention, if only our society were more tolerant and understanding of their quirks and foibles. But autists must reside in the world as it currently exists. Researcher

---

[26] Researcher Laurent Mottron and his colleague Michelle Dawson coined the term "normocentrism" to describe the research bias toward labeling all characteristics associated with autism to as "abnormal" or defective, even for differential development associated with strengths and talents. They have demonstrated through research that autists tend to outperform neurotypical controls in a variety of perceptual and pattern-recognition tasks. Yet most researchers report differential brain activation patterns as deficits and either ignore evidence of autistic strengths or label them as "compensatory of other deficits." (Mottron 2011)

Laurent Mottron focuses most of his work on exploring mental strengths associated with autism, but points out:

> *"One out of ten autistics cannot speak, nine out of ten have no regular job and four out of five autistic adults are still dependent on their parents. Most face the harsh consequences of living in a world that has not been constructed around their priorities and interests."*[27]

The Davis program offers tools for empowerment, to give each person the ability to exercise choice in his life rather than to be limited by a set of disabilities he seems to have developed along the way. Addressing the disabling aspects of autism does not in any way negate or undermine the strengths and talents that may also be associated with autism. On the contrary, the increased self-reliance, independent living skills, and social skills gained via a Davis program can also provide the means and opportunity for the individual to better develop their autistic talents—for example, to increase the availability of educational and career opportunities where particular interests can be further developed and expressed.

The State of Being Unoriented

When Ron Davis describes himself as coming from "the void," he is describing a mental state that might be described as *unorientation*, probably consistent with the most severe forms of autism. It is *un*-orientation rather than *dis*-orientation because the severely autistic child has not developed the ability to achieve a single or consistent state of perceptual awareness that can be associated with a feeling of normalcy or lack of confusion. If *disorientation*

---

[27] (Mottron 2011)

is the opposite of *orientation,* then a person cannot experience one without the other.

The state of orientation may also be connected to consciousness, metacognition, and rational thought. That is, an animal may have the ability to focus, sustain attention, and be keenly aware of its environment, as with a predator stalking its prey—but is it *oriented?* For the purpose of the Davis program, that is not enough, because Davis teaches the ability to be consciously and deliberately aware of and to control one's state of orientation.

The state of *unorientation* is not necessarily unpleasant.[28] It may at times be a state of pure sensory awareness, existing only in the moment, fully feeling, hearing, seeing all that is happening. If the environment itself is comfortable, if the perceptions and sensations are pleasurable, then it is quite possible that the unoriented person will be in a state of bliss. For the moment. Because the unoriented person does not have the ability to exercise control over his environment, or to think about past or future, to remember the sensation of pleasure when he is feeling pain, to recognize and understand his own existence as a separate and conscious entity.

On the outside, this is the person who fits the definition of classic, severe autism. It is the child who seems entirely unreachable, lost within his own world, unable to engage with or meaningfully interact with his parents or others who work with him. He does not engage because he doesn't know *how* to turn on that part of his

---

[28] In her book *My Stroke of Insight,* describing the impact of a left-brain hemorrhage, neuro-anatomist Jill Bolte Taylor articulated the feelings that accompanied her loss of the ability to regulate her thoughts. She wrote, "I watched my mind completely deteriorate in its ability to process information .... the essence of my being became enfolded in a deep inner peace." (Taylor 2008)

brain that would allow him to engage.

So we can see *unorientation* as a mental state that may be experienced by infants, but which is typically left behind with the development of intent-based consciousness and metacognitive thought.

When a facilitator works with a *disoriented* child or adult, the facilitator will be giving him a tool that will enable him to find his way home. It is the functional equivalent of a mental compass and the instructions on how to use it.

When the facilitator is working with an *unoriented* client, the person does not have any experience of home. That person needs more than a mental compass because he does not have the ability to recognize when his mind is at the spot where the perceptions he experiences have become normal. He can still be taught the skill of self-orientation, but it is likely to take much longer. First the facilitator will need to provide a mechanism that allows the person to become oriented without having to consciously think about it. Only after having spent a significant amount of time in that oriented state will the person be ready to develop the ability to recognize what orientation is, and to intentionally shift from a state of disorientation to orientation.

Alternative or Partial Orientation

A higher functioning individual on the autistic spectrum probably does not have the experience of occupying a void. On the contrary, that person may be very capable of engaging in highly directed, sustained, intensely focused activity or inquiry, even to the point of exhausting and frustrating others around him. An example might be a boy who is fascinated with all things having to do with buses, who has memorized the bus schedules and complete routes of every bus in his home town, whose first request on visiting a new city is to see a transit map, and whose day is complete when his father comes home and takes him out for a ride on a familiar bus route.

However, even a very high functioning autist may still feel a profound sense of disconnectedness. Eric Chen, a writer and computer programmer diagnosed with high functioning Asperger's at the age of 19, was able to complete mainstream education in Singapore without any academic difficulties or need for special intervention. But he describes his childhood as existing without consciousness, writing that even as a teenager, "I was still mostly in a state of sleepwalking. I was unaware of my own emotions, body and situational awareness."[29]

It is also possible that the internal sensations and thought processes of autistic individuals may be variable, and for some could represent an alternate type of "orientation." Davis found that to be the case with his dyslexic clients. He noticed that when he worked with a client who was adept at athletics, the person often seemed to be oriented, but nonetheless experienced great difficulty with making out words in print. Ron discovered that the dyslexic athlete often had a natural orientation point that was centered above his midline, but too far forward. That provided an excellent vantage point for the brain to engage in active pursuits, which typically involve moving one's body through space or focusing on and reacting to fast moving objects. However, it resulted in potentially

---

[29] From the web site iautistic.com at: http://iautistic.com/autism-myths-the-curious-incident-of-the-dog-in-the-night-time.php (retrieved July 6, 2011). Chen is the author of the books *Mirror Mind* (2005), *Autism & Self-Improvement* (2007), and *Star Child on Earth* (2010), which chronicle his own experiences with autism and his journey toward self-discovery.

distorted perceptions when both the person and the object of his focus were stationary. So Ron included a step for fine-tuning orientation that anticipates the possibility of the athlete's orientation, and provides a way for facilitators to correct it.

Of course, no athlete wants to give up their prowess as part of a reading program, and no one had to. The Davis program simply provides each person with the ability to recognize and intentionally control his orientation, including the ability to switch among two or more types of orientation. So the dyslexic athlete may actually experience improvement in his athletic skills, as he is motivated to explore the best orientation for his chosen sport, as well as to easily shift back to the best orientation for reading.

It is equally possible that the autistic musician has hit upon an orientation that is ideally suited for understanding and producing music, for coordinating elements of rhythm and spacing and tone and pitch as the sounds reach his brain, for easily and automatically remembering and reproducing long passages of music, for seamlessly integrating the knowledge of which keys or which strings produce a desired tone or effect. But if that musician cannot function effectively outside of his music, if he can engage for hours on end with his instrument but not even for five minutes with his parent, then whatever type of orientation he has is not complete.

Similarly, the hypothetical high-functioning autistic child with the fascination for all things bus-related may have figured out how to tune his brain to the setting that is right for studying and integrating the contents of a transit map or schedule, but his autistic difficulties reflect an area where orientation is incomplete.

It is a matter of semantics to decide whether the alternative mental state is an alternative form of orientation, or rather reflects a type of disorientation. In either case, it is an example of the brain efficiently performing its self-wiring task in areas where the autist is adept, but missing the needed connections for the social-behavioral aspects that are deemed autistic.

For that person, Davis Orientation Counseling supplies a missing piece. Davis Facilitator Ray Davis' first autistic client was a teenage boy who very much matched the description of the autistic musician above.[30] Ray's client (I'll call him Tyler) is an exceptionally talented pianist, but had no ability to engage with others outside his music. Tyler's mother doubted that Ray would be able to work with her son for more than a few hours during the course of a day. Nevertheless, she arranged for Ray to travel to her home in Michigan to begin to work with Tyler.

Tyler picked up on orientation immediately. Ray was able to give him the regular Davis Orientation counseling—the visually-oriented, mind's eye approach—and Tyler plunged into the Davis Autism Approach Program with the same intensity that he had previously focused on his music. Ray was exhausted; Tyler wanted to work with him ten hours a day without a break, and Ray had to be quite firm and persistent when he wanted to stop for a meal or to use the bathroom. But with that dedication, Tyler worked through all the Identity Development concepts in one week.

Because Tyler pressed so quickly through those concepts, Ray felt it was best to leave some settling-in time before moving on to the Social Integration phase of the program. Ray returned home to California, letting Tyler know that he could call whenever he wanted. Several months passed, and then Ray received a phone call. It was

---

[30] Ray Davis, who is Ron Davis' son, is also a Davis Autism Facilitator/Coach.

Tyler, wanting to share a new discovery: *"I can turn it off, Ray ... and I can turn it back on."*

For Tyler, being oriented allowed him to experience silence. Every moment of his existence had been filled with music, and the Davis program allowed him to turn it off. With that silence he was able to be comfortable in the company of other people. But music was still his passion, and by letting himself disorient when he was with his keyboard, he could continue to compose and immerse himself in his music. So for him, turning "off" the autism was the same as turning down the volume on a stereo playing incessantly inside his head—but turning it back "on" was to return to the world which gave him such joy.

That may not be what parents have in mind when they seek help for autistic children, but Tyler's observation sums up exactly what orientation is all about. It is the ability to control the mental state. The person does not need to give up or abandon any thought process or passion that has provided him with enjoyment in order to be part of the world of the non-autistic.

That is why the Davis program is not described as a "cure." The person does not sacrifice the ability to use his mind in ways he or others may associate with his autism. He just gains the ability to also use his mind in a different way when he needs or wants to participate in the non-autistic world.

Tyler gained that skill during his week working in his own home with Ray. Tyler's sudden insight, months later, that the ability to turn the autism (and his inner music) on and off was tied to his need to interact with others, and was a sign that he was ready for the final step.

Chapter 4

Davis Tools for Orientation

The primary goal of the Individuation phase of the Davis Autism Approach is to provide the autistic client with one or more of the Davis tools for orientation. Orientation is a necessary precursor to the rest of the program, so an individual who cannot be oriented would not be able to progress further. In many cases, the orientation technique is learned quickly and the client is ready to progress to the next phase of the program almost immediately. In other cases, it may be an extended process.

Davis Facilitators know from their training that the answer to the question, "how long will this take?" is always, "it takes as long as it takes." Each individual is different, and there is no benefit gained from trying to rush through a step, even if it were possible to do so. A high-functioning individual can be taught some form of orientation in less than an hour, and become quite adept at re-orienting himself with practice over several days. The same process could take several weeks with a lower-functioning child, especially if the child is nonverbal.

Opening the Door

In order to work successfully with a client, a Davis Facilitator must be able to create a relationship based on trust. One cardinal rule of any Davis program is that a facilitator will never work with an unwilling client. That does not mean that the autistic client must affirmatively ask for the program. It would be unrealistic to expect many autists to be able to understand what is being offered at the outset, or to make an informed choice about whether or not they desired a program.

But it does mean that a Davis Facilitator will not work with a client who is uncooperative or clearly resisting her efforts. Unlike some behavioral approaches to autism, a Davis provider will never use any sort of coercion, threats, or negative reinforcement to try to solicit cooperation.

Thus, when a facilitator first meets a potential client, it is important to lay a solid foundation for future work. As many autists are wary of strangers, and by definition are not strong with social skills, the facilitator must be extremely sensitive to the needs of her prospective client. This means that the facilitator must approach the client gently, with an open and patient manner.

Davis Facilitators are trained in specific techniques to aid them at this first meeting. To someone not familiar with autism, the facilitator's behavior might seem a little odd. A parent looking on from an adjoining room might see the facilitator walk into the room and sit down near the child without saying anything, seemingly making no effort to engage the child or to attract attention to herself. However, the facilitator understands that the child has probably noticed her even if he seems to be ignoring her. She knows to wait until she sees some signal from the child, perhaps a quick glance her way, as an indication that he is ready to allow more extended contact. The autistic child will respond positively to the facilitator's stillness. In this setting, it is important for the facilitator to let her client control the timing. To rush the process would risk engendering feelings of fear or intimidation, which in turn would stand in the way of further progress.

Once the client does acknowledge the facilitator's presence, she will explain briefly—in terms he can understand—who she is, and ask his permission to allow her to work with him. Again, that request will be made in a very simple manner.

Of course, things may proceed much more quickly with a high functioning autist. An adult with Asperger's is likely to have contacted the facilitator on his own. A high-functioning child may have been well-prepared for the meeting with the facilitator by his parents, and need little introduction. The key is that the facilitator will take her cue from the client; she will wait and observe so that she can match her rhythms to his.

The fact that the facilitator has specialized training does not mean that she will be successful in all cases. But there is a very high probability that a Davis-trained facilitator will be able to establish a rapport and a basis for working successfully with the client. Sometimes, if an autistic child is resistant to the facilitator, the family may choose a coached program, perhaps with the facilitator coaching a therapist or tutor who already is familiar to and accepted by the child.

Of course, sometimes it doesn't work out, and a decision must be made to forego the Davis program or at least wait until a future time when the individual may be more ready to accept the help that the facilitator can offer.

Davis Tools for Orientation and Self-Regulation Skills

Davis Orientation Counseling	*Relies on visualization skills; suitable for older children, adults, and picture thinkers*
Davis Alignment /Focusing	*Relies on kinesthetic imagination; suitable for younger children, individuals with limited communication skills, and kinesthetic learners*
Davis Auditory Orientation	*Relies on auditory experience; suitable for all learners of all ages, but can also be used as a means to bring about orientation with individuals with limited communication skills*
Davis Release	*A simple stress-release exercise, used by Davis Facilitators and given to all students*
Davis Dial-Setting	*A technique for developing self-awareness and the ability to regulate energy levels, as well as developing awareness of energy levels of other people*
Koosh Ball Exercises	*Simple exercises with tossed Koosh balls, used to fine-tune orientation and improve balance and coordination*

Teaching Orientation to an Autistic Individual

There are three primary routes to guiding a person toward orientation—one geared to visual imagery, another focused on sensory and tactile imagination, and the third based on an auditory stimulus.

The visual technique—*Davis Orientation Counseling*—tracks the method that Ron Davis discovered and used as a first step toward correcting his own persistent dyslexia at age 38, when he found he could stabilize his perceptions by changing the position of his mind's eye. It works well for most dyslexic individuals over the age of 8, and often can be used successfully with high functioning autists with good communication skills.

The tactile approach involves imagining and remembering the physical sensation of a pair of hands resting on the shoulders as a way of reorienting oneself. This is called *Davis Alignment* or *Focusing*.[31]

No Davis client will ever be given both the visual "mind's eye" Orientation Counseling and the sensory "hands on shoulders" Alignment at the same time. Although both approaches accomplish nearly the same effect, the feeling of being oriented is slightly different depending on the tool used. That slight difference doesn't affect the person's ability to stabilize perceptions, but it could be very confusing—and disorienting—to try to do both at once. Usually the facilitator will start with the

---

[31] The main difference between Alignment and Focusing is the complexity of the language used in instructing and guiding the student. Focusing was originally developed for use with young children ages 5-8 in a classroom setting, but would also be appropriate for an autistic individual of any age who has limited receptive language skills.

approach that seems best for her client based on a pre-liminary assessment. If the client later has difficulty with the chosen approach, the facilitator may switch to the alternate method, after first taking her client through a process to undo the initial training.

Because these techniques rely on the client's ability to follow a set of verbal instructions, they are not appropriate for an autistic child who has not acquired at least the receptive language skills of a typical pre-school age child. Receptive language means the ability to understand and follow simple instructions. It does not matter whether the child is able to speak coherently, as long as the child can understand and at least respond with a nod or head shake to the facilitator's instructions.

If an autistic child cannot follow the Orientation or Alignment/Focusing instructions, the facilitator may use Auditory Orientation. The auditory technique can be also be used in conjunction with the other forms of orientation; Davis Facilitators generally offer it to all their clients. In those cases, the facilitator will start with Orientation or Alignment training if possible, and then guide the client through the Auditory Orientation procedures after he has had some time to practice the primary approach.

Auditory Orientation involves listening to a recording of a reverberating tone played at regular intervals. When a person is properly oriented, he will hear the sound as emanating from the proper location for orientation: behind and slightly above his head, directly at the midline. The reason the tone reverberates is to enable the person to sense its position.

Humans are pretty good at identifying the position of a sound that is even slightly to the right or left of their midline, as sound from an off-center point will always reach one ear slightly ahead of the other, or be heard as slightly louder in the ear that is nearest to the sound. But when a sound is exactly midway between the two ears, it sounds identical to both ears, and there is no way for the brain to distinguish between a sound coming from the front and one coming from the rear.

In real life, people rarely notice this problem. For one thing, a real sound in a room will also reverberate or echo against walls and furniture. Though the sound itself may not give a clue as to whether it is coming from the front or rear, the subtle echoes of the sound bouncing off the furniture provide the extra information needed to identify the location of the sound.

Also, when a person hears a real world sound, he usually will react by turning his head toward the location he thinks the sound came from. If the sound is repeated, its source will then be in a slightly different position relative to the person's head, and the person will be able to hone in on the source of the noise.

But Auditory Orientation is an artificial situation, where the client listens to a repeating tone through headsets or earbuds. The headsets ensure that the sound reaches each ear at the same time, no matter how the person turns his head. The actual chime that was used to make the recording was suspended from a cord and reverberated about half an inch in either direction when struck. The reverberations generate a series of more muted tones that emanate from both the left and right side of the chime. That helps draw the person's attention to the sound, and provides the auditory clue needed to localize the position in space.

A person with good language skills can follow a set of specific instructions from the facilitator when going through Auditory Orientation, and that is often the procedure followed with autistic as well as non-autistic clients. However, the auditory method can also be used with a client who has no language ability at all, if he is willing to wear headphones or earbuds.

When a Davis Facilitator has a client who cannot be oriented through an approach involving instruction—or perhaps a client who is not yet ready to work with the facilitator—the parents can be provided with a take-home CD with the recorded tone. The parents will typically be instructed to allow the child to wear a headset or earbuds and listen to the CD—or to another device, such as a MP3 player—for as long a period in every day that the child is willing to listen. If the child does not like listening to the tone by itself, the tone can be recorded over a favorite piece of music that the family provides.

The process of orientation will take somewhat longer with this approach, because without instructions, the client will have to localize the source of the chime on his own. The CD was recorded with a device designed to accurately capture the spatial location of the tone. As it repeats at regular intervals, the mind's attention will be drawn to it, and eventually the person will naturally start to hear the tone from its proper position, and become oriented in those moments. For someone who has never been oriented, or is habitually disoriented, the attention may quickly drift away from that position—but the repetition of the tone will continue to function as a lure to bring the person back to a state of orientation. The more the person experiences orientation, the more he will become accustomed to hearing the tone in its proper position, and the easier it will become to remain oriented for longer periods of time.

If the child refuses to wear headsets or earbuds, Ron has designed an experimental, alternate method of delivering the tone to the child in a way that its position can still be sensed consistently. It would not work to merely play the tone externally, such as over speakers in the room where the child is playing, because the location of the tone would then change with the child's movements. For the auditory orientation to work, the source of the sound must remain the same, in relation to the child, no matter which way he moves or turns.

But it is possible for a person to hear sounds, clearly and accurately, without relying on a device attached to the ears. Hearing is simply a matter of tiny bones in the ear converting vibrations into neural signals; the vibrations do not need to come from the outer surface of the ears in order to be heard. So Ron developed a device that transmits the sound vibrations through another part of the body. To do this, he uses a tiny electronic device, similar to an MP3 player, with a pair of small transducers that function similar to speakers. The device is attached to a small self-adhesive pad, which can be affixed to the skin on a person's body. The sound vibrations then are transmitted through the skin and body and the individual has the sense of being surrounded by the sound. As the sound volume is low and the tone is intermittent, this is not an overwhelming experience; it is just an alternate way of enabling the child to hear a single repeated tone in a consistent way.

Ron calls his device a NOIT—Neural Orientation Induction Telemeter—and currently the unit is being tested with a small research group of parents of severely autistic children. The unit is very lightweight and can easily be placed on a child's back, worn under clothing, in a place where it is not likely to be dislodged by the child's other movements. It is still too soon to draw broad conclusions about the effectiveness of using the NOIT device, but as research continues, information will be available at the web site *www.noitresearch.org.*

Davis Self-Management Tools

In addition to the various approaches to orientation, all Davis programs include three other simple self-regulatory tools: Davis Release and Dial-Setting, and the Davis Koosh Ball exercises.[32]

Davis Release

Davis Release is a simple tool for relaxation and stress-release. Via a scripted exercise, the person is directed to intentionally tense their muscles, and then to relax them, and to focus on the feeling of relaxation. This feeling is labeled "release;" the person is directed to associate that feeling with the act of sighing. Later, whenever the person feels anxious or frustrated, he knows that he can take a sigh of *release* to let the feelings of tension leave his body, to be replaced by the feeling of calm relaxation.

Although Release is a technique specifically developed by Davis, it is very similar to stress release approaches that might be taught in a yoga class along with the concept of a "cleansing breath," and you could probably find many similar relaxation routines simply by searching the internet for "stress release" exercises. The Release technique is particularly valuable because of its simplicity.

Facilitators use this technique for themselves as well, and may take a sigh of release alongside their client, or as a reminder to their client—or, on occasion, because the facilitator is the person beginning to feel somewhat

---

[32] Like Davis Orientation and Alignment, these tools are described in full in Davis' book, *The Gift of Dyslexia.* (Davis and Braun, Gift of Dyslexia 2010)

frustrated.[33] This technique can be learned by other family members as well. With the shared understanding and vocabulary, it can provide an easy calming tool for use at home as well as during sessions with the facilitator.

Release is always taught in conjunction with Orientation Counseling, Alignment or Focusing, and will be generally used as a first step for re-orientating. When a facilitator is working with a client and the client is experiencing any difficulty, the facilitator will typically encourage the client to first take a sigh of release, and then to use his chosen orientation method to refocus his attention.

If an autistic client is nonverbal and relying on listening to the auditory ting recording, the formal teaching of release might be deferred until the client is better able to listen and follow instructions. However, the facilitator will be modeling release throughout her work with the client. A Davis Facilitator knows to use release as a tool for herself before she even enters a room to begin working with her client. It helps ensure that the facilitator will not be bringing her own outside tensions and anxiety into the realm of her work with each client.

Dial-Setting

Dial setting is a tool used to help a person regulate his own energy level, and also to learn to observe and respond appropriately to others around him. The client is taught to imagine a regulatory dial, such as a dial that might be used to control the volume of music, and to assign a

---

[33] The sigh may be a natural response to frustration in any event. Based on observations of subjects asked to work on frustrating, insoluble puzzles, one researcher concluded that "sighs are often unintentional expressions of an activity, plan or desire that has to be discarded, creating a pause before it can be replaced by a novel initiative". (Teigeh 2008)

different energy level to each number on the dial. The number 1 would correspond to being asleep—a 9 or 10 would be the level of highest possible excitement and activity—for example, how a person would feel while being chased by a tiger. The client is encouraged to settle on a number that represents his own energy level during normal, day-to-day activity. Usually this will be somewhere between 4 and 6.

With the dial, the client is first encouraged to be self-observant. The facilitator might ask, "Where is your dial now?" "Is that a good number for what we are doing?" "What do you think would be better?" "Please reset your dial to that number." Thus, a child who seems highly active and agitated during a work session with the facilitator might be guided to lower his dial from 8 (too high) to 5. The approach could be used the other way, to help perk up a sleepy person by raising the inner dial from 3 to 5.

The Davis client also learns to focus on others and estimate what their dial setting might be. For example, a child might be asked to observe other children on the playground who are actively engaged in play—perhaps their dials are at 7 or 8.

This exercise is used over time, and is especially useful for any individual who experiences difficulty in social relationships or whose behavior tends to annoy or vex others. Between the self-observation and the observation of others, it will help build and reinforce the ability of the person to modulate his energy level to be appropriate to their surroundings and in sync with others around him.

The exact language and the type of activities done with dial setting vary according to the age, developmental needs, and vocabulary of the client. For a client with autism, learning and understanding this tool could be very difficult. It involves the ability to think symbolically, and to assign an arbitrary number to an emotional or physiological state. It also requires self-awareness and the ability to focus attention on others and draw conclusions about their internal emotional state.

At the same time, this tool is exceptionally useful to the autistic client, and may in itself engender new insight, as well as providing a very simple and direct means of improving social skills. So Dial-Setting will definitely be part of the arsenal of Davis tools provided with an autism program. However, depending on the client's level of readiness, it may be introduced at a later stage of the program, perhaps after the client has been able to make a clay model of *self*, or perhaps after he has mastered concepts such as *time*, *order* and *sequence*. In some cases, an autistic client might not be able to understand the idea of a dial without those extra concepts, which will be given during the first part of the Identity Development phase.

Koosh Ball Exercises

The Koosh ball exercises are used to fine-tune a person's orientation and also to improve the person's balance and coordination. Typically, a Davis client will practice using his orientation or alignment skills while standing balanced on one foot and catching a Koosh ball that is tossed to him by a facilitator or other support person. If the client is properly oriented, it should be easy to balance for a short period and to catch a ball that is gently tossed his way.

As with the other tools, introduction of this exercise may be deferred until the autistic client is ready. If the client was not taught orientation by one of the instruction-based approaches, he will not be ready to use the Koosh ball exercise for the purpose of improving his orientation. He has not yet been taught to think consciously about his orientation, so he would not understand that part of the exercise.

But the Koosh ball exercise also works, over time, to improve a person's ability to coordinate mind and body, especially involving tasks that involve crossing the midline, such as alternating between right and left hand to catch the ball. The Koosh ball is used because it is lightweight and easy to catch; when tossed gently, it is unlikely to bounce back out of the hand of a person who is trying to catch it.

Orientation is all about harmonizing the brain's function, to enable the person to use his brain to perceive his environment in a consistent way, and also to be able to make the connections between thought and movement that often are difficult for autists. The facilitator will introduce a number of activities, such as standing on one foot while catching a ball in one hand, practicing catching balls in each hand, practicing catching a ball thrown from one direction first with the nearest hand and then with the opposite hand, and practicing catching two balls at once. Of course the exercises are modified as necessary to accommodate any physical limitations of the client, and will start at the client's level of physical readiness. If a person is not able to stand on one foot, the exercise can start with two feet on the ground. If the person cannot stand at all, the exercise can be done while seated. The goal is to do whatever is possible with the individual, with the understanding that with practice over time, abilities will improve. Variations can be introduced as appropriate to the client's needs and developing skills.

The Koosh ball activities will take place during short sessions, usually as part of taking a break from other tasks. There is no set timetable: the more the person practices with the Koosh balls over time, the more his mental and physical coordination skills will improve.

Chapter 5

The Importance of Self

The word autism is derived from the Greek root *autos,* meaning "self". It is somewhat ironic that the autist often has great difficulty developing self-awareness or understanding the very concept of *self,* or at least conceptualizing *self* in the same way that non-autistic individuals do. Emerging brain scan evidence reveals that autistic adults show different brain activation patterns than non-autistic control subjects when engaged in tasks involving thinking about self as compared to tasks related to thinking about others.[34] Autistic children are also somewhat less likely to use personal pronouns or self-referential gestures in communication than their non-autistic peers.[35]

Davis uses the term *individuation* to refer to the process of developing self-awareness. A person who is *individuated* can identify himself as separate from all

---

[34] (Lombardo, Chakrabarti, et al. 2010) (Frith and Frith 2008)

[35] (Hobson and Meyer, Foundations for self and other: a study in autism 2005) (Lind and Bowler 2009)

others. He functions as a single unit. His senses and perceptions can function in harmony and he has the capacity to be fully aware of his surrounding environment.

Developing Self-Awareness

A typically developing child will begin the process of individuation at about the time he starts walking, and become fully individuated by the time he is age three. The process is reflected in emerging language; the toddler will frequently express himself through words and phrases like "mine!" or "me do it" or "no!" The toddler has developed a sense of himself as apart from others, along with his own set of opinions and an urge to assert them.

The autistic child may share Ron's early sense of being everything and nothing at the same time—of existing, sensing, perceiving—but not of functioning as a cohesive and separate individual. A very high functioning autist might seem on the outside to be self-aware, as well as self-absorbed—but the quirks and nuances of his behavior can result from incomplete individuation. For example, he may have a habit of talking incessantly about a peculiar and highly technical area that he finds extremely interesting. His lack of awareness that most other people are bored by the topic stems from the inability to fully realize that he is not only separate from, but is also different from, the others around him. They do not share his interests. This characteristic is sometimes referred to as lacking "theory of mind"—that is, an inability to understand that others have beliefs, desires, and intentions that are different from one's own. But researchers now recognize that the autistic difficulty with imagining and predicting the processes of other minds likely originates with a weaker grasp and awareness of the workings of the individual's own mind.[36]

To develop a conception of self, a person must have the ability to perceive his surroundings in a consistent manner, and to integrate and harmonize perceptions and sensations as they are experienced. If perceptions are disrupted, a person can be easily fooled into losing track of where his own body begins and ends. An example is the rubber hand illusion. When a person's own hand is placed out of view, and a visible fake hand is stroked in synchrony with the hidden real hand for a minute or two, the person will usually start to experience the fake hand as being part of his own body.[37] If asked to close his eyes and point out the location of his hand, the person will point to the fake hand; and with eyes open, the person will flinch if the experimenter strikes the fake hand.

It only takes two minutes to fool a fully developed adult brain into confusing a fake hand with a real one. Thus, it is not hard to see that perceptions are important to developing body awareness in the first place. Ron Davis' own experiments demonstrated the direct effect that disorientation had on the accuracy of perceptions.[38] So it can

---

[36] (Lombardo and Baron-Cohen, The role of the self in mindblindness in autism 2011)

[37] To view this illusion in action, see *Rubber Hand Illusion,* http://www.youtube.com/watch?v=TCQbygjG0RU (Uploaded by newscientistvideo September 19, 2007; Retrieved June 10, 2011) or *The Rubber Hand Illusion – Horizon: Is Seeing Believing?,* http://www.youtube.com/watch?v=sxwn1w7MJvk (Uploaded by BBC Oct 15, 2010; Retrieved June 10, 2011).

[38] The impact on perception has been demonstrated with a series of experiments using a body-swap illusion, a variant of the rubber hand illusion, where 3D imagery is used to invoke the sensation that the subject is inhabiting a different body. When the illusion was created using a body the size of a Barbie doll, the research participants reported perceiving ordinary objects (a pencil

(continued on next page)

be expected that the person whose perceptions are inconsistent due to his lack of a stable orientation will also have an inconsistent sense of the limits of his own body.

Even with very high functioning autists, poorly developed body awareness is often observable through a clumsy or awkward gait or poor physical coordination skills. For example, author Eric Chen describes his childhood experiences:

> "I never looked at the world from inside my body. I was not 'in' me.
>
> "I did not know that I had a body. My hands did not belong to me, and I did not know that I have feet. I had no idea where my body parts were, unless I looked for them with my eyes. I was also not aware that I can control my body parts or precisely how to do that.[39]

A person must have a sense of body awareness in order to also develop a sense of integration of mind and body, and that sense of integration is necessary to conceive of an individuated self. Without the ability to orient, a person is unlikely to develop a complete and consistent sense of self.

(*continued from previous page*)

and the experimenter's hand)—as being gigantic. When the experiment was repeated with a different set of subjects utilizing a giant-sized artificial body, the participants judged ordinary objects to be much smaller. A similar effect was seen for the ability to judge spatial distance. (van der Hoort, Gutertam and Ehrsson 2011)

   [39] (E. Chen 2009)

Davis Orientation and Emerging Self-Awareness

When an autistic client gains the ability to orient by learning one or more of the Davis techniques, he will begin to experience his world in a new way. He will then begin to individuate. That will happen whether or not the person continues to the next step of the Davis program. Individuation is the natural result of consistent and harmonized perceptions. If a person can make sense of his world, and if his perceptions are consistent from minute-to-minute and from day-to-day, that person will naturally develop a sense of his own physical and mental boundaries.

However, the process of individuation could also be a lengthy and very messy process if one simply allows nature to take its course. When a typically developing toddler individuates, he will go through a phase expressing his will through temper tantrums, known to most parents as the "terrible twos." Along with the realization that he is his own person and that he has his own opinion will come rage whenever his opinion is violated, and frustration when large, powerful adults exercise control in violation of his opinion—for example, by refusing to buy candy for him at the supermarket.

The tantrum that comes with the toddler's emerging sense of self is different than an autistic melt down. The toddler's tantrum is tied to his growing ability to form an intention and recognition of causal relationships. He typically throws a tantrum because he wants something that his parents won't allow, or wants to avoid something that his parents insist upon. The tantrum will often subside very quickly if the toddler's demands are met. Of course, good parents know that it is a mistake to give in to the toddler's tantrums, but the toddler who is on a healthy path to individuation is developing more sophisticated ways of expressing his desires and is better able to regulate his own emotions over time. Because he has also developed the ability to perceive his world accurately and consistently, he will make connections between one event and another, and develop a sense of cause and effect. As he grows, he will experiment with alternate strategies, such as effective use of language and tactics such as flattery, begging or bargaining. The tantrums will subside.

The toddler's tantrum is fueled by an emerging sense of self and his ability to exercise control of his surroundings, coupled with anger and frustration when efforts to exert control are thwarted. The older autist will have the same response to an emerging sense of self, but the bigger the person is, the more damage he can do when venting frustration. Ron Davis was working on ways to orient autistic individuals long before he had developed a program to guide them once oriented. One of his early clients, a teenager, expressed her emerging sense of self by smashing every single window in her parents' house.

Most parents seeking help for an autistic child also want to see improvements in behavior. There is a difference between a child who fails to meet parental behavior expectations because he lacks the ability (the autistic child), and one who is both capable and defiant. But it will be difficult for most parents to see defiance as a sign of progress, especially if the defiance involves behavior that causes damage to property or injury to other people.

So it makes sense to help autistic children and adults come to terms with their newfound sense of self with a guide and a plan. Unlike a toddler, the older autist has the intellect to grasp and integrate concepts that are learned through a combination of explicit teaching and guided exploration. The same concepts that the toddler learns through trial and error can be conveyed to the older autist through an organized series of conceptual lessons, over a period of weeks rather than years.

Davis is not a program to teach or influence behavior, so there is nothing in Davis that will guarantee that the emerging individual will behave in accordance with parental wishes. On the contrary, for a teenager or young adult, a certain amount of resistance to parental demands is normal and to be expected.

But the Davis program can and does provide each client with the knowledge, wisdom and understanding needed to begin to make sound and age-appropriate decisions. Without the Davis concepts, it would be un-reasonable to expect a newly oriented and individuated twelve-year-old to be as capable and self-sufficient as other twelve-year-olds; the autistic child simply has missed out on years of life lessons that were experienced by his age mates. The older he is at the time of a Davis program, the greater the gulf between his experiential knowledge and what is expected of typically developing individuals at the same age.

The Davis program is aimed at filling that gap. This is done through the process of Davis Concept Mastery, a program combining clay modeling and environmental exploration, structured and sequenced specifically to meet the needs of autistic clients.

The Meaning of Mastery

The first step in the Concept Mastery phase of the Davis program is the modeling of the concept of *self* in clay. In many cases that can be done immediately after the autistic client has been given the orientation tools. However, some individuals may not be ready immediately, and a period of weeks or months may pass before the person has experi-enced life in an oriented state long enough to individuate. A delay would be more common for those individuals who were not able to learn orientation through an instruction-based approach, but instead relied on sustained listening to the auditory orientation tone.

Ron Davis believes that mastery is the truest form of learning. A person who has mastered an idea or concept will not have to rely on memory in order to call up or work with that idea. Instead, once mastered, the idea becomes a part of the person, something that is with him automatically, without the need for a conscious or effortful recall. It has become something innate, assumed, and taken for granted. Most of the skills or knowledge that are used by humans on a daily basis have been mastered.

A good example is the route that a person follows while traveling each day to work and back. After a while, the route becomes so ingrained in the person's brain that she is fully capable of getting into the car and arriving safely at work at the appointed time, all the while listening to the radio and thinking about things unrelated to the task of driving. At one time the route had to be learned, but over time it is simply something that the person can manage without conscious thought.

Davis also believes that in order to *master* some idea or fact, a person must experience it in three ways: as an observer, at the point of causation, and at the point of effect. Davis has assigned a name to each type of learning: *understanding* for information learned as an observer; *knowledge* for information gained through being at the receiving end, or experiencing effect; and *wisdom* for what is learned from creating or being at the point of causation.

The Davis approach to training facilitators is structured around the same concept. As part of their training, each Davis Facilitator will spend a week acting in the role of a client receiving a program (effect); a week acting as an observer of a fellow trainee providing a program to another in the role of the client; and a week performing the role for which she is training, as the provider of a program (cause).

The astute—or confused—reader will notice that the order of presentation of each of the three elements of mastery has varied in the previous two paragraphs. That's because it really doesn't matter in what order the process of seeing, getting, and doing takes place. In real life, it is likely that there will be a mixing up of the process in mastering complex ideas and concepts. A person will usually not be engaged in one type of learning exclusive of the others, but almost every participatory learning experience will probably include a little bit of all three.

Davis also believes that there can be no true learning without involvement of the creative process. That might just be a different way of expressing the idea that knowledge and understanding are not sufficient to attain mastery; the person must also have the wisdom piece before he can truly integrate the knowledge. To go back to the example of the experienced commuter: the worker could study a map or have someone else drive her to work every day, but the route is truly mastered only after she has driven the route on her own, probably several times.

These basic principles are at the root of all Davis methodology, and the path that will be followed with the autistic client through Concept Mastery. It is one reason that clay is used, as clay modeling provides the client with the opportunity to create the concept on his own.

It is important to keep in mind that a person can create without the need to be highly imaginative or original. When Davis was first working with dyslexic clients, that distinction didn't need to be made; dyslexics tend to be highly creative, out-of-the-box thinkers, who revel in the opportunity to do something in a unique and novel way. By contrast, many autists seem to be very concrete in their thinking and expression of ideas.

But Ron Davis himself made his first red dirt models at a time when he was still in the void. When he coveted his brothers' pocketknives and watches, he didn't want to model something new and different—he used the red dirt to fashion a copy of real world objects. As a child, Ron probably tried to make those copies as exact a representation of his brothers' possessions as his little hands could manage.

The modeling of the autism program is very largely guided and directed by the Davis Facilitator, or by a parent or other helper following the explicit instructions of a coached program. The client will be asked to come up with his own ideas for many of the models, but at the beginning the autistic client may need a lot of prompting to come up with those ideas, and his ideas may be simple and prosaic. As the client progresses, rather than becoming more imaginative with models, the autistic client will learn to construct "simplest form" models—that is, models using simple elements such as balls and arrows.

For purposes of the Davis autism program, the ability to use clay modeling to represent an abstract concept is more important than the artistry of the process. Simplistic models are an expression of the ability to engage in symbolic thought. Many autists tend to think and communicate in very concrete terms, so a shift to symbolic representation of abstract ideas can be an expression of profound growth. Of course some autists have exceptional artistic talent, and some may be fascinated with the opportunity to model real world objects in clay. But the end goal of the program remains a focus on the concepts represented, no matter how rudimentary the model.

Davis uses clay because it works. Clay is inexpensive, readily available, easily replenished, and can be used by children and adults alike. The non-hardening types of clay favored by facilitators are versatile enough so that the same clay can be reused to create models over and over again, but also firm enough so that particular clay models can be retained for reuse in later models, even if the process of completing all models takes many weeks.

However, clay is merely a tool. It happens to be the tool that works best for the greatest number of clients. Sometimes an autistic client will have a particular aversion to working with clay. That does not mean that the Davis program cannot be completed with that client; it just means that the facilitator will have to find a way to work around the client's aversion. Sometimes the client dislikes the texture, color or smell of particular clay, and another brand can be substituted. Some clients may not like the idea of getting clay on their hands, but will be happy to work with the clay while wearing gloves. Sometimes a different media needs to be explored—there is nothing inherent in Davis modeling that can't be accomplished with Tinkertoys or Lego blocks; it's just that most of the time, clay is much easier to work with.

Constructing a Model of Self

The Concept Mastery phase of the Davis autism program begins with the model of "self." As this is the first model the client will construct, the facilitator usually makes her own model as an example, so that her client can clearly see what is expected. She will ask her client to make a small clay figure, about two or three inches high, in the shape of a person. She will explain that the model will represent the client, saying, "the person is going to be you, and you will be using the model to show how you fit into the ideas."

Generally, a very simple model is made. If the model has two legs, two arms, and a head, it will suffice for purposes of the program. There is no particular need for the model to accurately depict the individual's appearance.

Once the model is built, it will be given a label.

Generally, the label will be the word "me," because "me" is the word that a person would use in a sentence when talking about himself. When the model is made, clay ropes are used to fashion the letters in the label: m, e. The word is laid out in front of the model.

Once the model is done, the Facilitator will lead the client through a very specific dialogue. The client will point to the model and say:

> *"You represent me. You represent every experience 'me' has ever had. You represent all of the knowledge, all of the wisdom, and all of the understanding."*

At this point in the program the autistic client does not have the ability to fully comprehend all of the words used in that sentence. Even an extremely high functioning and verbal client has not yet reached the parts of the program where the concepts of knowledge, wisdom, and understanding are fully explored. But a younger child or a lower functioning autistic teenager or adult may also be facing new vocabulary. It is not important that the autist understand every word at this stage of the program—the only concept that is important in the beginning is the idea that a clay model can be used to represent *self*.

The words representing other concepts are important at this stage because they will be repeated later on, throughout the program. With the model of *self*, the facilitator has introduced a pattern that will carry the client through the program, and will enhance his ability to integrate the concepts he will be given along the way.

Even though every model will also include a model of the spelled out word, the autism program is not intended to teach a pre-literate client to read. If the client does not yet read independently, then he needs to understand only that the letters represent the spoken words; the facilitator will help as needed with making the letters and laying them out. For the autism program, reading is not important—but words are. The simplest way to make a model of the sound of a word, as opposed to the concept it represents, is to use letters to spell it out in clay.

Typically, each model will also include a clay arrow pointing from the word to the part of the model that the word depicts. In some cases, when the entire model depicts a single unitary concept, the arrow is not needed. The arrow—which Davis calls a "dominant arrow"—is used whenever needed to indicate which part of the model depicts a meaning corresponding to the word. As the client progresses through the program, sometimes a single model will be used to portray multiple concepts; the dominant arrow is then essential to help differentiate the ideas encompassed within the model.

After the first model is made, the facilitator will guide the client to represent three separate aspects of the self: *body*, *mind*, and *lifeforce*. This is done by making each word in clay, and using arrows and clay circles to indicate the part of the model that represents each concept. At each stage the client is also given a definition and follows a script with this pattern:

[Pointing to the model]:

*"You represent my **body**, my physical form."*

[Pointing to the word]:

*"You say **body** meaning physical form."*

The same script will be followed for each and every concept introduced through the remainder of the program: the client will create a model of a word and a concrete description of what the word represents, and when done the client will speak out loud to the model. The model represents the concept itself; the letters "say" the word which has the meaning that is represented by the model.

If the client is not verbal, the facilitator will work with whatever communication skills the client does have. In order to do the Davis program, the client must have the receptive language skills needed to understand and respond to the facilitator, but if the client himself cannot or will not speak, then gestures may substitute for spoken words.

The three aspects of *self* (or "me") are defined as follows:

Body   physical form

Mind   thought process

Lifeforce   the urge to be who and what "I" am

Individuation is a process of coming to terms with the idea of "self" as a person, and that begins with integrating the concepts of body, mind, and lifeforce as three separate but integrated aspects of the individual person.

The terms "body" and "mind" are easy to define and understand. In clay, the body can be depicted merely by setting out the letters of the word "body" with a clay arrow pointing to the model of self. "Mind" is depicted by the creation of a thought bubble—a loop of clay connected at one end to the head of self, with bits of clay placed within the loop to represent thoughts.

The term "lifeforce" will not be found as a single word in most English dictionaries. One dictionary defines the two-word phrase "life force" as "the vital force or impulse of life; one's source of vitality, spirit, energy, and strength."[40] Philosophers, cognitive scientists, and theologians might debate endlessly over the concept of "life force"— whether it exists as a separate entity; its relationship to concepts such as consciousness, spirit, or soul; its genesis and source. But the goal of the Davis program is simply to present concepts in their simplest

incarnation, in order to give the autistic client all that is necessary to function in life, but no more than is needed. An unnecessary or superfluous concept is something that potentially causes confusion; it also would prolong the program and occupy time that is better spent focusing on what is necessary.

The concept of *lifeforce* is necessary because it embraces the concept of *urge*. An *urge* is the foundation of emotion and motivation, and is the source of the energy that drives every action and decision in life. At its most basic, an urge is the instinctual drive to seek pleasure and to avoid pain. If a person is to understand himself, to recognize what drives him to do anything at all in life, then he will need that concept of *lifeforce* as the urge to be what and who he is. Complete exploration of the *urge* concept

---

40 life force. Dictionary.com. Dictionary.com's 21st Century Lexicon. Dictionary.com, LLC. http://dictionary.reference.com/browse/life_force (accessed: October 06, 2011).

does not take place until later in the program. During the Individuation phase, the concept is simply represented by a circle of clay formed around the standing model of self, and an arrow pointing to that circle.

After the client has modeled "me," and used that model to depict *body, mind,* and *lifeforce,* the facilitator will bring him back to the single word "me," and have him say:

[Pointing to the word "me"]:

"You say me meaning every experience 'me' has ever had. All the knowledge, all the wisdom, and all the understanding. You represent my urge to be who and what I am."

The first model of self will usually be retained for use during the remainder of the program, as "self" will be part of every model made in the Identity Development and Relationship Concepts parts of the program. Whenever additional models of self are made, the process of telling the model what it represents is repeated.

When the client has completed the model of self and its three aspects, he has demonstrated that he is fully individuated. He is able to use orientation to ensure that his perceptions are consistent and that his senses are integrated as he experiences the world. In modeling self, he has shown that he has developed an awareness of what he is in relation to those now stabilized sensory perceptions, and an awareness that he is a unique being, separate and apart from others. The *Individuation* phase of the Davis program is complete.

Chapter 6

Identity Development:
An Overview

The next phase of the Davis Autism Approach is Identity Development. With individuation, the person is able to recognize his own *self* as an individual, separate and apart from others—but he has not been given any understanding of what that *self* is or can become. He knows that he *is*, but he does not yet know *who* or *what* he is or *where* he is headed. In the final stage of the Davis program, he will be able to explore social relationships—but before he can do that he has to solve the deeper mysteries of *self*.

To do that he must first come to terms with the world that *self* inhabits. Then he must understand his inner world of thoughts and emotions, and finally he must be brought to the place where he can occupy a role of responsibility within his world. Only when all that is in place will he be ready to move on to the next step of forming relationships with fellow human beings, as their equal.

The Concept of Identity

Identity development is not simply a form of intervention for autistic individuals, but rather a normal and continual process that every human goes through. It begins as soon as the child individuates, but it continues as the person matures and incorporates new experiences, new ideas, new skills, and new knowledge into his being. It complements the Davis concept of *mastery*, because as something is mastered it becomes a part of the person, hence a part of his identity.

The concept of "identity" is inherent in the words used to express the representation of *self*: every experience the person has ever had, all the knowledge, all the wisdom, all the understanding, and the urge to be who and what he is.

Our identities are composed of multiple facets or layers, which are added and incorporated as we go through life. Each new experience, each new role or responsibility will add to that identity. An experience that is prolonged or experienced as meaningful is likely to have a bigger impact on identity than one that is transient or short-lived. For example, if a person moves to a new country and learns to speak a new language, that change may have a profound impact on his identity, because language, culture, and nationality are powerful influences. Each new facet will develop on its own, because that is the natural response to having a new experience.

The autistic client who comes to the Davis program already has an identity—he has a set of experiences, he has some level of accumulated knowledge, he has urges that motivate him in some manner. But it is an identity that is missing an important element that is part of the identity of individuals who are considered "normal" in their development: that part which allows the person to understand and function effectively within their community environment. We can refer to that element as the core identity. Without it, the individual will not be able to integrate and benefit from new experiences, simply because he cannot truly make sense of or exercise control in his world.

The Identity Development phase of the Davis program is aimed at building the core identity, adding a new layer of understanding and integration of knowledge. Because it is additive, it does not change the underlying identity—it simply fosters an important phase of development that did not take place naturally because of the individual's autistic state. But it is also foundational: it is building a central or *core* identity that can bind and connect the pre-existing elements of identity, and provide the groundwork in which future personal development will take root.

Because identity continues to develop through life, completion of the second phase of the Davis program does not complete the process of identity development. On the contrary, it simply provides a stronger foundation for the future, natural lifelong development that will inevitably take place. With that foundation, the autist will likely experience a richer set of life experiences in the future. He may travel on his own, attend university, pursue a re-warding career, marry, have children, and do all the things that so-called "normal" teenagers and adults do to grow and experience their lives to the fullest extent possible. Most importantly, he will develop a sense of his own inner need for self-expression, and will be able to articulate, formulate and pursue goals that enrich his life and give it meaning.

The Davis Concept Mastery Process

The Identity Development phase of the program is a highly structured, incremental exploration of specific concepts, accomplished through dialogue with the facilitator, clay modeling, and explorations of the environment. Each step begins with the facilitator offering some words of explanation, and then guiding the client with suggestions, questioning, and prompting. The facilitator will always prompt the client to supply answers, rather than merely teaching or instructing. In addition to invoking the creative process through such guided questioning, this practice helps ensure that the client actually understands the ideas the facilitator wishes to convey. The client cannot merely mimic or echo the facilitator's own words; only when the client is able to express and explain the concepts on his own will he be ready for the next step.

Generally the discussion will proceed to the creation of a clay model to illustrate whatever concept is being discussed. Every model will include the clay model of *self*, because without *self* in the picture, the client may not internalize the concepts. With *self* he understands that the concepts learned apply to and affect *him*; without *self* the models could be seen to merely depict some set of rules or ideas that are unrelated to him. Based on ideas developed from dialogue with the facilitator, the client will choose what to model in order to represent each concept.

During most of the first construction, there will also be three versions of the model created, one with *self* at each position that is integral to learning: as an observer, at the point of cause, and at the point of effect. Those are the elements that lead to mastery, and allow the client a virtualized sense of having something happen to him, observing, and creating each concept. The clay modeling cannot replace real world experiences. Instead, its purpose is to prepare the client for the real world experiences when they occur.

After the initial model, the facilitator will spend time with the client exploring the environment to apply the concepts discussed to real life observations and situations. If the facilitator is working full days with the client, they might spend an entire afternoon with the explorations. If the facilitated sessions are shorter, the client may also spend time at home between sessions, exploring with his parents or with another helper or aide.

Usually, the final step for each concept is to complete a "simplest form" model in clay. Generally the facilitator starts by making her own "simplest form" model, and asking the client to copy what she has done. This is done with very rudimentary models, using clay balls, clay arrows, and very simple object models. With the simplest form models, it is easier to build on one model to create the next concept, and to see the connections between the models. They also help the client to recognize that a concept learned in one setting will apply to other settings. As the modeling progresses, reliance on simplest form modeling can speed up the process; at some point the client will abandon the imaginative modeling altogether, and begin with the simplest form. At the end of the Identity Development phase, some of the models will be quite complex. The simplest form practice will then make it much easier for both client and facilitator to monitor what has been included in each model and to keep track of additions and modifications.

Every time a concept is modeled, whether in the imaginative form or simplest form, the model will also include the letters of the word that represents the concept. There will be only one word on the table at a time, so that each model can be clearly understood to represent the single concept being addressed.

At the completion of each model, the facilitator will ask her client to point out the essential elements of the model, and conclude by pointing to the model and identifying it in the same way as was done with *self*. First, the client will speak to the model, "*You represent [concept], meaning [definition of concept],*" and then he will repeat the same step with the word, pointing to the letters and saying, "*You say [concept], meaning [definition of concept].*"

The repetition of the script means that the client will soon know it by heart, and it will become part of his thought process. It also will give the client a sense of orderliness and control. The client will be able to anticipate the next step, even without being told, because the same pattern of words is spoken with each model. If the client has weak verbal skills, the repetition will probably help to strengthen them, at least with respect to the use of the Davis vocabulary. When the client identifies the part of the model and speaks its meaning, that process allows the facilitator to monitor and to be assured that the client's attention is focused on the mastery task and that he understands his own model.

The Davis Concept Mastery Sequence

Davis has created three basic series of conceptual development, termed "constructions." Each construction begins with a "root" concept, which is a simple idea founded on a natural law—something that happens in nature with or without human participation. The three root concepts are *change, continue,* and *energy.*

Ron Davis' own identity can be seen in the selection and structure of these concepts. Ron is the product of a severely autistic childhood, and as an adult he has been an engineer, an educator, and a sculptor. So he chose a set of concepts that fit his own intellectual leanings, and of course chose the medium of clay modeling as the means to express those concepts. He considered it vital to create a foundation based on the simplest ideas and to build upon it, applying his engineer's penchant for stability to array the concepts and their order of presentation. He selected the first series of concepts because of his lifelong love of mathematics, as the series of ideas explored are also the essence of understanding math.[41]

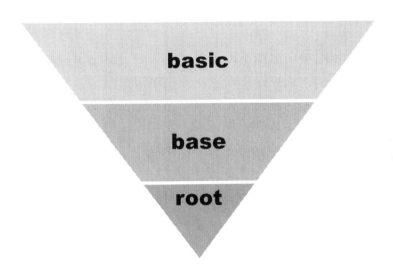

In each construction, after the root concept, the autistic client will be introduced to a "base" concept. The "base" is derived from the way we, as humans, experience the root concept. The root, *change*, leads to the base concepts of *before and after, cause and effect,* and *consequence*. From the root *continue*, the client will move to the base *survive;* and from the third root *energy,* the client will discover the base *force.*

Each construction also includes a third concept level,

---

41 (Davis, *Nurturing the Seed* 2009, 37)

which Davis terms "basic" concepts. A *basic* concept is that which reflects knowledge derived from the *root* concept. Since *knowledge,* as Davis uses the term, is something that is gained from experience, the *base* concept represents the experience which leads to the knowledge reflected in the *basic* concepts.

Davis sees each construction as forming an inverted pyramid, with the simplest, root concept at the bottom, and the base and then basic concepts occupying wider positions above the concepts from which they are derived.

In the first construction, *change* leads to *consequence,* and *consequence* leads to *time, sequence,* and *order vs. disorder.* In the second construction, the path is from *continue* to *survive* and then to *perception, thought,* and *experience.* And in the third construction, *energy* leads to *force,* which in turn leads to *emotion, want, need,* and *intention.*

The first construction focuses largely on the outer world as experienced by *self.* It is through this construction that the autistic person transcends his world of chaos and is able to make sense of his surrounding universe.

The second construction revolves around the inner, mental world, and the third construction is focused on the emotional world. Through these explorations, the individual develops a sense of how his inner world relates to his outer world. The three constructions can also be seen to mirror the three aspects of *self*: *body, mind,* and *lifeforce.*

The autistic client will take each construction one at a time, in precise order. Every step of the first construction will be modeled before moving on to the second construction, and the second must be done from beginning to end before tackling the third. Generally, very young children will hit a point at which they can go no further, simply by virtue of their level of maturity. Davis Facilitators have worked with autistic children as young as age four, but only up to the point of modeling consequence. If a six-year-old child—autistic or not—is able to complete all models in the first construction, that is a significant accomplishment. That child may not be ready to tackle the second construction until he is somewhat older. That delay is not a function of the child's autism, but of his maturation process. The younger child simply has not yet reached the stage at which any child is likely to have developed the capacity for abstract thought required to move on. In general, a Davis Facilitator would not expect to be able to do a complete program with an individual under age seven—and of course, in some cases, a child would have to be much older before being ready to embrace and understand the more advanced concepts.

However, the six-year-old autistic child who is oriented, individuated, and has worked through the base concepts of the first construction would be on par with normally developing six-year-old children. The goal of the Davis program is to put the autistic individual at the same level as a normally developing pre-teen or adolescent. If a child is younger, the likely approach will be to take a break of weeks or months when the child seems to reach a plateau, coming back to the next step later when the child seems ready. In many cases, the parents will be able to take over, with coaching as needed from the facilitator.

After a Davis client has completed the third construction, he will move on to modeling "common" concepts—a set of complex ideas that are derived from two or more of the root concepts. Those are *ability*, *motivation* and *control*—all concepts that underlie a person's ability to function as an independent and self-directed person.

The final Concept Mastery step is to model the advanced concept of *responsibility*. The "advanced" concept is one which links together all of the other concepts—root, base, basic, and common. When the client has modeled

the advanced concept, he will have attained a sophisticated degree of self-understanding, possibly more
insightful than many non-autistic individuals have
managed.

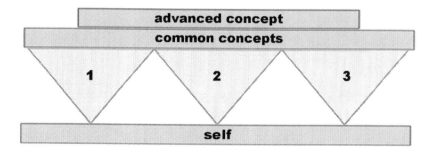

Davis sees the common and advanced concepts as
bridging concepts—ideas that are supported by and span
the three constructions upon which they rest. In this
fashion, the new concepts are added and integrated, so
that *self* has built the foundation for a new and powerful
layer of his identity. Unlike the autist who was once
overpowered by a sense of chaos and confusion, the
emergent individual's identity is now one of competence
and confidence. This is not due to a process of teaching,
but rather to one of mastery and integration of new
knowledge, wisdom, and understanding.

The final step of Identity Development is to move away
from the modeling, and put the newly acquired information into action. Most often this is done with an
"establishing order" exercise—the client is given the task of
taking responsibility for some part of his life, and establishing order within that zone. For children, this typically
can be their bedrooms or a part of the house or room that
is theirs, such as a shelf or chest of drawers. With that
final step, the individual is able to truly incorporate his
knowledge into his functional, daily life.

Chapter 7

The First Construction:
From Change to an Ordered World

After reading the previous chapter, you may feel that you have a good sense of what the Identity Development phase is all about—and if all you are looking for is a generalized picture of the Davis program, then now is the time to skip ahead to the chapter on Social Integration. This book is not an instructional manual, and reading the next several chapters with a more detailed breakdown of each and every concept is not going to give you the sort of information you would need to attempt this program on your own. On the contrary, if you tried to use this book as your primary resource for a do-it-yourself program, you would very soon find yourself in serious trouble. You would have a list of ingredients without explicit instructions on what do with them.

But Davis Concept Mastery is also a journey of discovery, exploring concepts and ideas and relationships and universal truths. The following chapters should provide the non-autistic reader with a greater insight as to the way these concepts tie together, and their importance to the emerging development of the autist's awareness and understanding of his world. These concepts usually are discovered piecemeal and haphazardly as typically developing individuals grow through childhood and into adolescence. As such, they are often taken for granted, without much thought or analysis. By looking more closely at each concept in turn, you may see some ideas in a new light, as well as getting some idea of what the autistic individual, who doesn't yet have the sense of these concepts, may be thinking and feeling.

If you have an autistic family member or student who is going through the Davis program with some other person in the role of facilitator or coach, then this book will also serve as a good reference as to what they are doing and learning at each step of the way.

The autistic person has inhabited an inner world of chaos. For a lower functioning individual, chaos is all that has ever been experienced. A higher functioning autist will have carved out his own islands where his world makes sense to him, but he still has the impression that those islands are surrounded by chaos. He has essentially become a prisoner of whatever areas of safety and sensibility he has managed to construct. No matter what the level of function, the chaos stems from a sense that the world is an unstable and unpredictable place. The first construction will eliminate the chaos, by taking the autist from *change* to *order*.

The Root Concept

Change—something becoming something else

> "*I never knew that things changed. Everything in my life was all separate pieces. I thought that when the leaves were green and then yellow, that the green ones fell off and the yellow ones were there. I never knew it was the same leaf! I thought that the tall candle was replaced with a short*

melted candle—I didn't ever know it was the same candle. Even the carpet we are standing on is changing—everything is changing!"

> – Report of an 18 year old girl ("Marla") during a Davis program[42]

Most autistic individuals tend to be highly resistant to change in their life.[43] One common trait of autism is an insistence that things remain in whatever order the autist has settled upon, whether it is the way he insists that his toy action figures be lined up on a shelf, or the specific sequence in which food is served at the table.

The resistance is grounded in fear. The autistic person's world is one of utter unpredictability. He is not able to correlate one set of experiences with another, to realize that a different route can be used to arrive at the same destination, or to anticipate a positive outcome from a deviation from routine. Instead, any change, or even the threat of a change, may give rise to uncontrollable feelings of panic, often triggering withdrawal or a meltdown.

---

[42] Reported by Stacey Borger-Smith, based on a conversation with a client working with her husband, Lawrence Smith. Both Stacey and Lawrence are Davis Autism Facilitator/Coaches and Training Supervisors.

[43] Researchers have found that autistic children have difficulties representing and understanding changes over time. (Lind and Bowler 2009), citing (Boucher, et al. 2007). Kanner described "an obsessive desire for the preservation of sameness" as being a key characteristic of autism, and observed, "The patients find security in sameness, a security that is very tenuous because changes do occur constantly and the children are therefore threatened perpetually...." (Kanner, The Conception of Wholes and Parts in Early Infantile Autism 1951)

So it makes sense to start the process of identity development with the root concept of *change*—a "root" concept because it is founded in natural law. It is something that happens all around, whether or not there are humans to observe or instigate it. Leaves turn from green to yellow to brown and fall off of trees, flowers bloom and later die, daylight turns to night.

Like other root concepts, *change* is also an abstraction that cannot actually be seen by a person. A person sees the result of change—he can see what came before and what came after, but it is not possible to see the moment of change. When 18-year-old Marla thought that short candles appeared magically in the spot once occupied by tall candles, it wasn't because she missed *seeing* the point of transformation. It was because she missed making a mental connection between the fresh and spent candle, between the green and yellow leaves. She did not grasp the existence of an unseen influence forming a link between matter in different states, between past and present.[44]

Explaining the Concept:

When working with a client, a facilitator will begin with a verbal explanation of the concept, giving examples of the meaning of change and explaining that change is happening all the time, whether we are involved or not. The facilitator will give examples, perhaps illustrating them with concrete actions in the room, such as switching a light on and off, filling and emptying a cup of water. ("The

---

[44] The conceptual connection between changing states over past, present, and future has been described as "diachronic thinking." Various aspects of this thought process become habitual in typically developing individuals between the ages of seven and twelve years, but are not understood in the same way by autistic subjects. (Boucher, et al. 2007)

cup was full, now it is empty—a full cup becomes an empty cup, something becomes something else.") When the client seems to be getting the idea, the facilitator will ask him to provide his own examples, providing guidance as needed.

Creating a Model:

After the client has provided several examples, a model will be constructed. The change model will have five parts—there will be the model of self, two "somethings" in different states, an arrow pointing from one to another, and the word "change" spelled out.

These are the essential elements that will be contained within every Concept Mastery model. *Self* is always part of the scenario, because Ron Davis realized early in his work that, without the inclusion of self, it was possible for a client to understand a concept, but fail to apply it to himself and his own life. Ron had been working with a facilitator trainee who was using the modeling of consequence to help an ADHD child address behavior problems.

The child seemed to get the idea when applied to other people and things, but his own behavior continued to be reckless, in seeming disregard of the inevitable results. It was only when the concept was modeled again with "self" in the picture that the child got the message that *his own* behavior was part of the cause/effect chain of events.

As the primary purpose of the concept modeling in an autism program is identity development, *self* is the most critical part of every model. If *self* isn't there, the ideas cannot be incorporated into the identity. Without *self,* the clay modeling might help an autist better understand how the outside world works, but he would be unlikely to fully appreciate that the concepts apply to "me" and govern the decisions and actions that "me" takes.

The arrow is the symbol used in all Davis models to show a transition—that is, to show what is happening in the scene. It represents some sort of movement through time or space. It is a simple and intuitively understood symbol, but important as an essential grammatical element of the clay-language of Concept Mastery.

For the first "change" model, the "something" (which becomes "something else") can be anything that clearly portrays the concept. It is common for clients and facilitators alike to choose to model seeds growing into plants, or kittens becoming cats. Perhaps Marla might have modeled a tall candle becoming a short one. As long as the relationship between the two models is clear enough to see that one has "become" the other, the model will work.

Exploring the Concept in the Environment:

"Today we are studying the concept of change. Outside we could not help but find change everywhere we went! First we saw dozens of milkweed plants showing the beginnings of blooms: quickly butterflies caught our eye, blooms on the ash trees

*beginning to fade, grass and weeds growing taller
and taller. And then, walking just up the meadow
were a pair of geese marching their babies to the
pond. Something becoming something else."*

– From Davis Facilitator Cathy Cook

When the client has finished the model, the facilitator
will spend some time guiding the exploration of real life
examples of change in the environment. The client and
facilitator might take a walk outdoors, or explore change in
indoor environments like the home or a local café. If the
facilitator is working with the client in short sessions, the
client may go home and spend time with his parents
pointing out examples of "change" along the way.

For example, one boy's family regularly dined out, but
the boy always insisted that his family eat at the same
restaurant. He would throw a tantrum if the family wanted
a different restaurant, so they always ate at the same
place. After his session with Davis Facilitator Yvonne
Wong, the boy made the connection between "change" and
the family dining options. For the first time, he asked his
mom what other restaurants they were considering, and
participated in the family's choice to finally try a new and
different eatery.

That does not mean that merely modeling change will
transform the autistic family member into a model of
flexibility. It is human nature to cling to habits that give
pleasure, and it is quite common for typically developing
children to also have a favorite food that they want at
every meal, or a favorite article of clothing that they want
to wear every day. The autistic child who resists eating
vegetables is unlikely to become a broccoli lover simply
because his parent points out that eating it would be a
"change."

But with the concept of *change,* the family has a new shared vocabulary. While the autistic person may still cling tenaciously to many old habits and preferences, the *fear* that triggered the panic and meltdowns will dissipate. He will understand that *change* is the normal state of affairs, that everything in his world can and will change, and he will be able to integrate more and more change into his life over time.

When the facilitator feels that there has been enough time with exploring change in the environment, she will guide her client to make a second model.

Completing the simplest form model:

The second clay model is a "simplest form" model. Here the facilitator will guide the client to simply model two clay balls, one of which will be flattened or squished. The model will be the same, but instead of the client's own illustration of a "something," the idea will be represented through the use of the clay balls. With the completion of the model, the client will also follow the routine of pointing to the model and saying, "You are *change,* meaning something becoming something else." The client will then point to the word and say, "You *say* change, meaning something becoming something else."

The Base Concepts

The next step is modeling of the base concepts that come from the root *change*. A "base" concept is one derived from the way a person experiences the root concept. As noted above, the root concept is something unseen. Although a person may think that he is able to observe "change," what he really sees is the result of change. Exploration of base concepts means explorations of the aspects of change that individuals can directly observe or where they can have a participatory role.

The base concepts which stem from *change* are *consequence, cause* and *effect,* and *before* and *after.*

Consequence—something that happens as a result of something else

> *"I lived in my own world, with very little aware-ness of the outside real world around me. The things I made from dirt and water became a part of the world I lived in. I could bring outside ideas into my world by creating them from the dirt and water. The pain in my world came mostly from the daily beatings by my father. I did not like being beaten, so I didn't like my father. One day I made a model of my father from the dirt and water, and when it had dried and hardened, I smashed it back into dirt. This became a daily occurrence—every time I was beaten I made a model of him and then smashed it back into dirt. My older brother also hit me, so I made models of him and smashed them back into dirt. I didn't like any of the people that hovered around the edges of my world, so I made models of all of them, and smashed them back to dirt. Without an under-standing of what was occurring, I was actually*

creating models of the concept of 'change.'

"Over time, the models of my father began to include the act of the beatings. My models began to have more detail, and models of myself were included. Eventually the models became scenarios which included what had occurred before, during, and after the beatings. Again, without an understanding of what was occurring, I was creating the concept of 'consequence.' Through the creating of the models, including myself, and adding additional details, the concepts were becoming functional. I was beginning to think with the ideas. I was bringing an understanding of the outside world into my world.

"Like magic, when I was thirteen years old, the beatings stopped. The concept of 'consequence' had become a part of my identity. I either stopped doing the things that would cause a beating, or I took myself out of the environment where a beating could occur."

– Ron Davis[45]

As with the previous concept, the modeling of "consequence" begins with an explanation and conversation between facilitator and client, setting forth the definition and examples, and is followed with a model that the client creates. The subject of the model could be a depiction of something that arose from the discussion with the facilitator. It could be based on the scenario that was the subject of the initial *change* model, or it could stem from an idea that originates with the client.

---

[45] (Davis, The History of Concept Mastery and Symbol Mastery 2003)

With *consequence*, the model will also include an element depicting causation—the "something else" that results in the changed "something". Additionally, in this model *self* will be included in a role other than observer, either as the instigator of the change, or the person directly experiencing the result of change. This shift of role is important, again, in order to support the incorporation of the idea of *consequence* into the identity. Ron needed to build and smash models over and over again before he recognized that there was something in what his model of *self* did that triggered his father's violent reactions. The Davis autism client will be following a similar path, though the subject of the model will now be something neutral or positive, such as a plant growing as a result of *self* pouring water on the seedling.

Again, the modeling is followed by explorations in the environment. Now, when looking for examples of change, the facilitator and client will also think about or speculate as to the reason or cause for the change, so that each example can be framed in terms of *something* (for example, melted ice cream) that happened *as a result of something else* (the ice cream was left in a dish in a warm room).

The facilitator will then return to the client's model, and the same scene that was used for the first depiction will be recreated with *self* in two other roles, as an observer, and at the effect point (or the cause point, if effect was the initial model).

This exercise will be followed by the creation of a simplest form model, using the two clay balls. Here, the model will depict *self* stepping on one of the clay balls, thus putting self at the point of causation for the change of the ball from round to flat. Placing *self* at the cause point in the final model for *consequence* sets a foundation for the development of a sense of control over the environment, and ultimately a sense of responsibility.

The client once again follows the routine of speaking to the model, identifying the concept and its meaning, and then the word.

The impact of mastering the idea of *consequence* can be profound. Without the idea of consequence, autistic individuals are often simply unaware of or unable to make a connection between what they do, and what happens to them or around them in their lives. The discovery that their own acts can and do influence the acts of others, as well as the state of their environment, is tremendously empowering. Facilitator Stacey Smith reports that she repeatedly sees her clients start to insist on doing things for themselves—for her clients, the verbal expression of the integration of consequence into the identity may be the oft repeated phrase, "I do it!"

The reaction is not always positive at first. Facilitator Gale Long relates the story of a little girl who kept pushing the garage door opener to explore the idea of consequence. The next day she had a meltdown, throwing things, flinging pennies, and smashing every clay model—and then shouting "This is consequence!" After an auditory orientation session, the girl calmed down and commented, "That was lots of 'bad' consequence, wasn't it, Miss Gale?"

Marcia Maust had a similar experience with a 9-year-old girl, whose mom was doing a coached program under

Marcia's guidance. The little girl had been sent home from school one day for misbehavior. The following day, she intentionally misbehaved, and was sent to the principal's office, where she asked to go home. Instead, the principal sent her back to class. Once there, she slapped her teacher, and then exclaimed, "Now, can I go home?" That was the first time in her life that the little girl saw herself as the cause of trouble.

Even though such negative behaviors are frustrating to parents, they are a normal part of developing the connection between one's actions and the reactions of others. Gale realized that her client needed more facilitated time exploring consequence in positive ways before being ready to move on to other concepts. Marcia suggested that her client's mom try offering some small reward as an incentive for good behavior at school. That worked, and the girl's behavior in school improved. Part of the learning process is to test limits, to explore bad consequences as well as good.

Again, these are behaviors that typically developing children usually express as toddlers. The advantage of a facilitated series of lessons is that there is an opportunity to redirect the behavior in the course of explorations. The negativity is usually short lived, as the individual becomes more confident of the connection between his actions and expected results, and realizes that positive results are preferable to negative ones.

This illustrates one key difference between the Davis approach and behavioral approaches to autism such as ABA (Applied Behavioral Analysis). Ron Davis believes that when the reason for a particular behavior is eliminated, then that behavior will stop. However, the Davis program overall is aimed at personal growth, not specific behaviors. One aspect of normal human social development is that some of life's lessons are learned through conflict and resistance; certainly that is an essential facet of the road to independence. With Davis, it is important for teachers and family members to consider the reasons underlying undesired behavior. The child or young adult who is intentionally testing limits is engaged in an experimental process to observe and learn the consequence of his deliberate actions. Once a child has manifested the ability to think in those terms, it is no longer necessary for adults to constantly supervise or attempt to prevent undesired behavior; instead, the adults can guide behavior by being consistent in their response.

Cause—something that makes something else happen

Effect—something that is made to happen

> "Under the continuous flow of happenings
> The effect of a cause becomes the cause of another effect...
> But it is a world full of improbabilities
> Racing toward uncertainty."
>
>   – Tito Rajarshi Mukhopadhyay[46]

After the simplest form model of *consequence,* the next step is to identify *cause* and *effect.* Those two ideas were included and incorporated within the idea of *consequence,* but it is also important for the client to explore each idea separately.

To model *cause,* the existing simplest form model used for *consequence* is left in place, but the accompanying word is changed. The facilitator begins by providing the

---

[46] (Mukhopadhyay 2003, 201) Reprinted by permission of Arcade Publishing, Inc.

definition of the word *cause*, and guides the client to lay out the letters of the word. The client places the dominant arrow to point to the model of self stepping on the clay ball. All steps of Concept Mastery are completed. The client repeats the routine of pointing and speaking to the model: "You are cause, meaning something that makes something else happen"—and to the words: "You *say* cause, meaning ...." Then the facilitator provides the definition of the word *effect* ("something that happens as a result of something else"), the letters of the word are laid out, the dominant arrow is moved to point to the flattened ball, and the client again speaks to the model and to the word to cement his understanding.

With these models, one value of the simplest form model becomes apparent. Models of real life circumstances such as growing trees or broken toys provide room for creative application of the concepts, but can result in complicated models that are hard to fathom. Sooner or later some clients will manage to create models that seem to clearly depict consequence, but run into trouble on the artistic end when trying to sculpt a depiction of the cause.

With the simplest form models, the subsidiary ideas

from the main concept are easy to model, and because the same model is retained throughout, it is easy to see and understand the relationships among the concepts. *Cause* and *effect* are two parts of the idea of *consequence; consequence* is the sum of those two parts, incorporating the *change* of the initial model as well.

After modeling cause and effect, the client will again spend time with his facilitator exploring the environment, looking for examples of cause and effect. For example, they might stand at a controlled intersection and watch the cars when the light turns red and then green again. The cars stop as a *consequence* of the light turning red; the red light is the *cause,* the stopped cars are the *effect.* When the light turns green, the *consequence* is that the cars will drive off; the green light is the *cause,* the movement of the cars is the *effect.*

Before—happening earlier

After—happening later

The next step is mastery of the concepts of *before* and *after.* These also are two concepts already embraced within the idea of *consequence,* but now the idea of passage of time is introduced. The same process followed with *cause* and *effect* is repeated, this time with the dominant arrow pointed at the cause point of the model to represent the idea of *before* ("happening earlier") and at the effect point to represent the concept of *after* ("happening later").

The modeling will again be followed by real world exploration, perhaps by going back to the same intersection to identify *cause, effect* and *before, after* in the same series of events. To an autistic person, a linear understanding of time may be an entirely new idea. The autist may have always experienced his world as a series of random and unconnected events, with no consistent idea of the passage of time. The idea that a *cause* always precedes an *effect* in *time* may be a new revelation, which will bring a greater sense of predictability to his world. The understanding of his own role in the concept of *consequence* is integral to the development of a sense of control over his environment.

The Basic Concepts

The next step is to address the "basic" concepts derived from the root *change*—that is, concepts representing knowledge derived from our experience of change. We experience change as a consequence, and consequence encompasses the ideas of cause and effect, and of before and after.

Those experiences lead to the ability to create and establish a sense of order over the world, through understanding of the concepts of *time, sequence, order,* and *disorder.*

Time—the measurement of change in relation to a standard

Without an understanding of the concept of time, the autist is consigned to live simply in the present. He exists, he senses the world around him, he is aware of repetition in his life, but he is without the understanding needed to be able to plan, to anticipate, and to predict. He may sense a flow of time, but he doesn't understand time as something that he can manage or use as a means of gaining control over his life.

The human perception of time is inconsistent. We all have the sense that hours fly by quickly while we are engaged in enjoyable activities ("time flies when you're having fun"), and the span of ten minutes can seem agonizingly long when we are sitting on a bench waiting for a bus to arrive. But our response to that elongated bus wait is often to check our watches repeatedly—or these days, our cell phones—we know that the clock time is the "real" time no matter what we are feeling, and we rely on clocks and mechanical timers to alert us in situations where we think we might otherwise lose track of time as our attention wanders.

The autistic experience of time has probably been much more fluid, with the sense of passage of time distorted not only by disorientation, but also simply by the fact that the autist doesn't notice the passage of time when he is not attending to what is going on around him.

The Davis client has created the essence of the concept of time with the *before* and *after* model while exploring *consequence*. That is, the client has seen that the concept of *change* is something that entails the passage of time. When *something* is becoming *something else*, there is also a transition from earlier to later, though the duration of time represented by the change arrow can be very different depending on the nature of the change.

But to understand the passage of time is not the same as understanding *time* as it is used as a regulating force in modern society. Here we are not talking about time as a property of change that simply flows along with the change, but *time* in the sense of a second, a minute, an hour, a day, a week, a month, a year. Time that can be labeled and measured, and which comes with a commonly understood meaning.

Davis defines a *basic* concept as one that relates to the way humans interpret and derive meaning from their simple experience of the *base* concept. So for "time" that means adding the concept of *measure* to the simple experience of *before* and *after*. To *measure* means to compare something that is unknown to something that is known. The something that is known is a *standard*. For example, a kilogram is a standard unit of weight, as is a pound, but pound and kilogram represent two different standards. Whichever standard is chosen, the mass of the object will be the same. But it can be measured in kilos or pounds because both are known standards.

The mastery of *time* is achieved the same as other concepts: the Davis Facilitator initiates a conversation with her client, using examples, questions and dialogue to prepare him for the creation of the next model. A series of clay models are made, all with the new word—*time*—and its definition. After the first model, the facilitator works with the client exploring the environment to gain a better, real world experience of the concept. The client returns for more models, making sure that there are models depicting *self* in three settings: as observer, as the instigator of cause, and as experiencing effect. For each model there is always the routine of speaking to the model and word—identifying *self,* telling the model its meaning, telling the word its definition. And after the client creates a series of models employing his ideas as to the type of change depicted, there is a return to the simplest form model.

The definition of time is *the measurement of change in relation to a standard.* So the *time* model will include self, change, and two other elements: a representation of the standard, and a representation of the measuring device. The measuring device will be depicted twice: once at the *before* point of the model, and once at the *after* point, and the model will also depict the change in the measuring device corresponding to the elapsed time.

For purposes of the Davis program, the autistic client will explore the two different standards that govern the main ways that we measure, record, and discuss units of time, and the meanings that we attach to those measures. One standard is the daily rotation of the earth on its axis, a standard that gives us, from nature, the length of one cycle of day and night. Smaller units of time, such as hours, minutes, and seconds, are derived by breaking up the day/night cycle into fractional segments.[47] A model showing time in the context of the earth rotation standard will need to have a model of a rotating earth, and a model of a device to measure the passage of seconds, minutes or hours—usually a watch or a clock. The underlying change depicted will be something that happens within a shorter time span, always less than a day.

The other standard is the rotation of the earth around the sun, which in nature sets the length of a year, as well as causing the changes experienced with the four seasons throughout the year. So a model of change depicting that standard would include the earth and sun; and a measuring device geared to tracking months or years, which would be some sort of calendar. For those models, the change depicted will be something that happens gradually over a period of weeks, months or years—for example, a model of a baby changing into a standing child.

The final steps of mastery of the *time* concept are the simplest form models. Because the two separate time standards measure different kinds of change, there will be two simplest form models. The first is a model based on the already familiar squashed-ball *change* model, which will be augmented to include a model of a rotating earth and clocks at the before and after position. The second

---

[47] A "second" can also be derived by measuring the fluctuating states of electrons in an atom. Atomic clocks are keyed to the standard based on the atomic properties of cesium. However, over an extended period of time, atomic clocks do not keep pace with the earth's rotation, due to the fact that the earth's spin is very gradually slowing down, increasing the length of a day by about a second every few years. To solve that conflict, atomic clocks are reset with the addition of a "leap second" when needed, thus establishing that the earth's rotation remains the dominant standard for counting seconds.

simplest form model uses a ball of clay to represent an egg, and model of a small bird in the *after* position; the standard is shown with a model of the earth rotating around the sun, and calendar pages are used to depict the form of measurement.

Mastering the concept of *time* can make a significant difference in the ability of adults to lead independent lives. Davis Facilitator Cathy Dodge Smith worked with a 26-year-old woman with Asperger's who could not hold down a steady job (I'll call her Amy). Her mother reported that the first change she noticed during the program was that Amy arrived on time to a lunch date; she had always been at least an hour late before. After her program, Amy found full-time employment in a setting where she supervises others, and is now fully independent and self-supporting.

Sequence—the way things follow each other in time, amount, size, arbitrary order, and importance

"I continued modeling in the back yard, but now the models were showing a different kind of scenario. The models were still very simple but would clearly show different ideas like the passage of time or the sequence of events.

"Prior to this, my universe was the universe of everything and nothing at the same time. There was no separation of individuals, every thing and every one was just one. When I was modeling the beatings, I separated myself from the everything. So then there were two things, me and everything else. In the modeling of 'sequence' the other things began to separate into individuals and things. From the modeling of the ideas, I was making it possible for myself to 'think' with the ideas."

- Ron Davis[48]

The next step of the first construction is the modeling of the basic concept, *sequence*. The first part of the definition of *sequence* is "the way things follow each other," so the facilitator will introduce the new idea of *follow*. This is an idea that the client has already been exposed to in explorations of *before* and *after*. So the foundation for the first part of the sequence concept—"the way things follow one another *in time*"—is already in place, and the simplest form model can be used as a starting point.

However, in order to clearly model a "sequence," each model will need at least three parts. With only two parts (before and after), the model is depicting a pair of events

---

[48] (Davis, Waking Up 2005)

but not necessarily a sequence. For a *sequence* model, there must be a middle as well as a beginning and an end. In terms of clarity of the model, this will become important when the client models the remaining aspects of the definition: the way things follow each other in *amount, size, arbitrary order,* and *importance.* So a third clay ball will be added to the simplest form time/change model: first, the round ball, then the self stepping on the ball, and then the squashed ball.

The facilitator will discuss and explore each type of sequence with the client in turn, and the client will make separate models for each, following all of the steps of Concept Mastery. Each separate model will be retained for later use after each type of sequence has been discussed.

The concepts of *amount* and *size* will probably be easy for the client to grasp and to model, as those are probably already ideas that he is familiar with, even if he has not considered the concept of *sequence. Amount* could be represented simply by a number of clay balls—one ball, two balls, three balls. *Size* could be represented by three clay blocks, one small, one medium, and one large. Here it is apparent why the sequence must have at least three points, so that the client can discern that there is a pattern.[49] If the clay blocks were ordered from medium to large to small, there would be three blocks on the table, but that wouldn't be a *sequence.*

Arbitrary order is explained as man-made order, a sequence that someone has decided upon and we all agree to follow. The facilitator will explain that arbitrary order is used as a way of managing the process when more than one person needs to do something, such as a school time-table, the family morning routine, the order of letters in the alphabet, or the order in which food is brought out in the restaurant. This concept is very important and can be a revelation for an autistic person.

It is very common that the autist has gotten by in life simply by trying to memorize different routines or series, as he is unable to puzzle out the reason why things proceed in a specific order. He either takes for granted that things are the way they happen to have been first presented to him, or he believes that there is some sort of reason for the process that is outside his understanding. An autist will frequently cling to a specific routine and become upset at any deviation precisely because he cannot understand the source of the routine.

So with the idea of "arbitrary order" the autist is first introduced to the idea that sometimes people act or do things in a certain way for no particular reason except to get along with one another, and he is also introduced to the idea of "agree" as a basis for social connectedness. That idea might be difficult for the client to grasp at first, as it diverges from the other models. The other sequences

---

[49] Research studies have shown that autistic individuals are often quicker to visually discern patterns than non-autistic control subjects. (Soulières, Dawson and Samson, et al. 2009)

modeled relied on a continuing flow from smallest to largest (or largest to smallest), from least to most (or most to least)—with the middle object always something in between the other two. The *arbitrary order* model can break those rules, and it can be impossible to discern a pattern. For the first time, the autist must look outside the *things* that are sequenced to find the pattern, which stems not from the things themselves, but from the societal need to establish agreed standards.

That draws again on the idea of a *standard*, which was part of the *time* models, so it may be that the client and facilitator will explore the notion of standards as applied to arbitrary order. For example, different languages use different alphabets. In some, the letters may be quite similar, but be arranged in a somewhat differing order. The alphabet is a standard for writing in that language. The order is arbitrary, arranged simply to aid individuals in learning the alphabet and in arraying words and lists in a consistent way.

The final type of sequence is one based on *importance*. With this idea the facilitator can also introduce the idea that importance is relative, subject to change, and something that can be self-determined. *Importance* means being of significance or value. The facilitator will ensure that the client understands that a sequence of importance can change depending on our feelings or circumstances. Like the arbitrary order model, there may not be a clear pattern to order of *importance*. But the difference here is that the determination is made individually, based on the person's own preferences or beliefs.

An understanding of the subjective and changeable nature of importance will help the client when there are unexpected changes of routine in his own life. When circumstances change, a new sequence of importance needs to be created and adopted. Without that understanding, many autistic individuals are baffled and overwhelmed by such changes—in their eyes, the rule set they had come to depend on had been changed, and whatever new process came into being seemed capricious and unpredictable. With *importance* there is a new tool for analysis.

Of course one outcome of the understanding of *arbitrary order* and *importance* is that the autistic person may realize that he has his own opinions about sequences in his life, and he may start to assert those opinions. Long-standing household routines might be challenged. If the Davis client begins to deliberately analyze the practices in his own home and at school with these concepts in mind, he is likely to question which fits under the umbrella of *arbitrary* and which is derived from a ranking based on *importance*.

All things that exist, and all things that happen, exist and happen in one or more of the forms of sequence. The facilitator will work with the client to ensure that he fully comprehends and understands that fact. For an autistic person who has lived in chaos, or who has clung tenaciously to established routines out of fear of falling into chaos, this is a profound revelation. Everything in his life has a sequence. Rather than hundreds or thousands of rules to be committed to memory, there are only five different types of sequence: time, amount, size, arbitrary order, and importance.

When the client seems to truly understand this idea, five separate models will be brought back into one, so there is a single model of *sequence* which embraces all five ideas. A very complicated and confusing world has been reduced to a system that can be portrayed and understood in a way that can be counted on the fingers of one hand.

Order—things in their proper places, proper positions, and proper conditions

> *"With my universe newly separated into individual pieces, it was clear that everything and everyone that existed, existed in some place, and also existed in a position in that place. I was making rudimentary models of order. Everything that exists had a beginning and will have an end, when it will no longer exist. Therefore everything exists within its own time frame—its continuum. Where something is, within its time between beginning and end, is its condition. As a mentally deficient teenager I was creating my ability to think with these ideas by modeling them with red dirt and water.*
>
> *"Order is the natural enemy of chaos, and when I gained the ability to think with order, the chaos disappeared from my universe."*

– Ron Davis[50]

The next basic concepts to be mastered are *order* and *disorder*. These concepts are a natural next step from the exploration of *sequence*, which is the exploration of one scheme for placing things in order. The next concept will provide a different and more complete perspective. A sequence is linear, representing an essentially two-dimensional type of order. Mastery of the concepts of *order* and *disorder* provides an overview that applies in three dimensional space.

The concept of *time* is also integral to the understanding of *order/disorder*, because there is a temporal

---

[50] (Davis, Waking Up 2005)

element inherent in the definition as well. Whether something is in a state of *order* or not may depend on a factor of time, or changes that occur with the passage of time.

To understand that idea, it is first necessary to consider the meaning of the word "proper," which is part of the definition of *order*. Proper means, "according to what is correct or prescribed for a particular situation or thing."

Something is in *order* when it is in its proper state. *Disorder* means the opposite—the thing is not in its proper state.

There are three aspects of a thing's state that must be evaluated in determining order. One is *place*: the location of the thing. All things that exist will occupy some space. If a thing is in its *proper* place, then one aspect of order is satisfied. For example, we can imagine a coffee cup resting on a table top.

Another closely related consideration is an object's *position*. The *position* is the way in which something is placed or arranged in space, such as whether it is lying flat, leaning, or upright. If a thing exists in a space, it must also occupy some *position* in that space. For example, the possible positions of the coffee cup might be upright, inverted, or lying on its side.

The third aspect to consider is a thing's *condition*. The condition is the state of something, especially with regard to its appearance, quality, or working order. Is our coffee cup clean and empty, or filled with a beverage, or is it dirty? Is the cup intact, or is it cracked or broken?

Condition also includes a temporal element. All things that exist, exist in time as well as in space. Every object exists within its own time continuum; that is, each thing has a beginning and end, a before and an after, and each thing occupies some point in the flow of time and change. So *condition* also includes the state of the thing in time.

That is important because what is *order* at one time may be *disorder* at another.

The definition of order is things in their proper places, proper positions, and proper conditions. To constitute order, all three factors must be met.

Disorder is a dichotomy of order. Disorder means things not in their proper place, and/or not in their proper position, and/or not in their proper condition. If any one aspect is not proper, then there is a state of disorder.

Because everything exists in time, and time is the measurement of change, then what is proper can and will change, and it will change with time. If we go back to the coffee cup, and imagine it is sitting upright on the kitchen table, half full of coffee, we will need to know something about the time condition to determine whether the cup is where it should properly be. If someone is seated at the table near the cup and eating breakfast, then the cup is likely in its proper place, position, and condition; the cup is in a state of *order*. But if no one is at the table, and the coffee in the cup is cold, then it is likely time for the cup to be taken from the table to be washed. Because of the passage of time, the cup is in a state of *disorder*.

The Davis client will create models of order side-by-side. Because disorder is a dichotomy of order, it cannot be modeled or understood without the example of order also in the model. Similarly, the order model will need the contrasting images of disorder to make sense. The clay model for order and disorder will need to have a model (or models) of *self,* and four depictions of some object, one which is in order, and three which respectively show an improper place, position, and condition. The dominant arrow will point to the object that is in order for the word "order." After that word is mastered with the usual procedure, the word "disorder" will be substituted, with the dominant arrow pointed at the section of the model depicting the three forms of disorder.

The simplest form model for *order* and *disorder* will only depict one type of disorder. It will return to the basic construction of *self* and a clay ball, except that this model will have two models of *self.* One *self* will have the ball in hand, whereas the other will have lost the ball—a representation of *disorder* because the ball is not in its proper place and condition.

Like other steps of Concept Mastery, the client will spend time with the facilitator looking for examples of *order* and *disorder* in the environment. The client will not be asked to try to create order of his own at this phase of the program, as that is an exercise reserved for the end of the Identity Development phase, after the client has mastered other important concepts. Nonetheless, several facilitators have reported that their clients spontaneously began to use the *order* concept in their lives at this stage of the program.

One facilitator was working with a young boy at his family's vacation house. After finishing the model, he got up and created total and perfect order in the living room, without input or help from anyone.[51] Another child, a girl, finished the first construction, but halfway through the second construction went home and asked her mother to help her create order in her bedroom.[52] From those accounts we can see that with the modeling of the concept of *order*, the client will have attained enough knowledge to be able to create order in his own life, if he is so inclined.

However, the translation of knowledge to action may take more work, and the remainder of the Identity Development phase of the program is designed to fill in those pieces. At this phase the client should have a foundational understanding of the concept of *order*, but he may not yet see it as his personal job or responsibility to influence or create order. Exploration and mastery of a concept is not enough, by itself, for the concept to be incorporated into the individual's identity. Rather, these concepts provide knowledge that will support an ability to exercise control; but the client may still need more time to gain the skills needed to fully utilize the new knowledge. Many clients will not be able to integrate and use the initial concepts until they have fully explored the concepts yet to be introduced.

The modeling of *order* and *disorder* completes the first construction. The client, who once perceived his world as chaotic and dreaded any disruption to his tenuous sense of stability, has now learned that *change* itself is part of the natural order of things. He has learned that all things

---

[51] Reported by Davis Autism Facilitator/Coach and Training Supervisor Gabriela Scholter, of Stuttgart, Germany.

[52] Reported by Davis Autism Facilitator/Coach Tina Guy, of Nelson, New Zealand.

are a product of a stream of change, that the passage of time is the way we measure change, and that the standards of measurement we use are based on the regularity of some cycles of change. He understands the idea of sequence, and has the ability to evaluate any set of objects or series of events to determine whether a sequence—a regular pattern—exists, as well as to understand and adapt to sequences that are arbitrary or subject to change. And he has a very simple and direct, three-part analysis to recognize and clearly define order in his world. He can see the concept of *disorder* as being partnered with *order*, often simply reflecting a temporary state of change. So the first construction has led him out of chaos into an ordered, regular, and far more predictable world.

The remaining concepts are geared to giving him the ability to function more effectively within that world, to make the transition from being an observer to an active participant. Once he has mastered all of the concepts, he will be ready to begin the process of translating his understanding to skills that can be incorporated into his daily life.

Chapter 8

The Second Construction:
A World of Experience

With the first construction, the client experienced a set of connected concepts allowing him to make sense of the external, physical world. Everything that happens around him can be understood in the context of change, consequence, time, sequence, order, and disorder.

But the autist also lives in an internal, mental world. One characteristic of his autism may be an inability to distinguish his mental world from the external world, to know the difference between his thoughts and subjective perceptions, and reality. The outside rules don't govern the mental realm. In the mind, memory can restore things changed to the way they were before, and take us back to times long passed. Our thoughts may arrive all at once in a jumble of different ideas and impressions; thinking is not bounded by systems of sequence or order.

The model of *self* consists of three parts: body, mind, and lifeforce. The second construction focuses on *mind*, starting with the concept of *continue,* leading to *survive,* and culminating in an exploration of *perception, thought,* and *experience.*

The Root Concept: Continue (Remain the Same)

The model of the first root, *change*, established the basis for the existence of something. All things that exist have a beginning, and exist as a consequence of something else.

The idea of *continue* starts with something that already is existing. As a root concept, it is something that arises from nature, derived without human interpretation or intervention. Thus the clay model will include *self* only in the role of observer.

The definition of *continue* is simple: "remain the same." Even though the condition, place, or position of each thing will change, the thing itself will *continue.* For example, the leaves on a tree may change color and fall with the change of seasons, but the tree remains. A car may be driven about from place to place, sometimes going fast and sometimes stopped, and it may get dented or scratched— but it *continues* to be a car.

As with the other models, the client will spend time working with the facilitator and exploring the concept in the environment. He will first make a model based on his own representation, and later make a simplest form model under the guidance of the facilitator. Since *continue* means *remain the same*, the client's own model will simply depict some object that is the same on both sides of the transitional arrow connecting them. The simplest form model is also quite easy: it will have *self* as an observer, two identical clay balls, and a clay arrow signifying the flow of time from one to another. Unlike change, where one ball was squashed, here the two balls are the same.

Davis Facilitator Tina Guy relates the story of a twelve-year-old girl that I'll call Holly. Holly's mother had attended every session along with her daughter, and modeled each concept along with her. One night before bed, Holly asked, "Why do I have to grow up, Mum … I won't be your little girl anymore?" Her mom responded by pointing out that we all change, but that we also *continue* as self, and that her daughter would always *continue* to be her little girl. It was a huge breakthrough for that family for Holly to even be able to express her feelings in words; the mother was grateful to know that the Davis program had provided a vocabulary and a set of concepts to allow her to reassure and support her growing daughter.

The Base Concept: Survive (Continue as Self)

A base concept is drawn from the way we as humans experience the root concept. Our experience of the concept of *continue* leads directly to the concept of *survive*—to continue as self. However, to the autistic person, the continuity of *self* may not be intuitively obvious, simply because he has not had the same conceptualization of *self* during his childhood development.

There really is only one way to model the concept of *continue as self* using the clay vocabulary that has already been developed, so in this instance the client will make only one model. The model simply needs to have two clay representations of *self* and a transitional arrow, to indicate that the identical *self* is in the before and after position on the continuum. Of course, as in other steps of Concept Mastery, the client is also spending time discussing the concept with the facilitator, and exploring examples in his environment. For example, a bird in the tree is *surviving;* it

is building its nest and continuing as itself. A puppy is *surviving;* it is growing and changing, but it is still a puppy, and continuing as itself. The lady in the shop is *surviving;* she is going about her work and continuing as herself.

With the second construction, there will generally be no need to model *self* in the different positions of the cause, effect, and observer points of view. Because *survive* and the remaining concepts are about *self,* and the internal thought process and awareness experienced by *self,* the model of *self* is no longer outside the concepts or events depicted. Rather, in this construction, every model is about *self* and the way *self* functions. In some models there may be more than one *self* depicted, to represent the different states of *self* as he moves through time. But there is no longer a need for *self* to occupy different roles within each model.

In other words, the first construction was focused on things that happen outside of *self,* so it was necessary to establish a role for *self* in each of the models. Without that, one couldn't be sure that the client would relate the concepts about the outer world to his own personal experience, and incorporate those concepts into his identity.

But moving forward, the concepts are things that happen within *self.* The *condition* of self while experiencing these concepts may be an important part of the model, but there is no separate role, because *self* is always *self*.

And of course that is the key lesson learned with the model of *survive*: *self* may grow and change and adapt; he may wear different clothes, be wet or dry, or in good health or ill—but he is always *self*. Even if he feels different from day to day, even if there are times when he feels the desire to be alone and retreat into the safety of his autistic world, he is still *self*—but merely *self* in a different state of mood.

Basic Concepts: Perception, Thought, and Experience

Perception—external awareness

The next step is to model the basic concepts that stem from the root, *continue*, and the base, *survive*. The first basic concept to be modeled is *perception*.

With the modeling of *survive,* the client has established the existence of *self,* and that *self* is continuing. The next concept is the idea of other things existing outside of self. That concept is intuitive for neurotypically developing individuals, but the chaotic internal world of autism makes it difficult to sense the boundaries between *self* and the external world. In the realm of autism, it may all be the same.

In order for a person to be aware of something existing outside of *self*, he must perceive it. Perception is the way that things that exist outside of *self* are brought inside of *self*. Thus, the clay model will include *self*, an outside-existing thing, an arrow depicting the movement of the outside thing toward self, and a thought bubble showing the perceived thing existing within *self's* mind. As with other Concept Mastery steps, the process begins with a dialogue between facilitator and client, exploring the concept to be modeled, and is followed by the client fashioning his own model.

The facilitator will begin by discussing visual perception—the idea of *seeing*—and the arrow in the model will represent the process of sight. The physical object itself is not transferred into the mind of self, but self's eyes are capable of sensing the light waves bouncing off of the contours of the object, and in that way a picture of the object is created in the mind of the person who has seen it.

Following the model, the facilitator and client will explore the environment. At first they will continue to explore visual perception, perhaps by looking at real world objects, with the facilitator encouraging the client to describe what he has seen. Later, the facilitator will expand the discussion and activities to explore other senses—hearing, touch, taste, and smell. The facilitator may introduce games or puzzles based on these senses; for example, she may suggest that the client try to guess at an object while he is blindfolded, or the object is otherwise concealed from view. Can he identify an orange by its smell? A pencil by its shape and texture? Can he figure out what is causing various sounds in his environment? This part of the program can be a lot of fun.

As with other steps of Concept Mastery, the exploration of the concept will conclude with the creation of a second, simplest form model.

This phase of the program can be revelatory. At its heart, autism is the manifestation of a divergence in the way the brain processes and interprets perceptual input. The autist simply perceives and experiences the world differently than his non-autistic counterparts. It is possible that he has hyper-acute sensitivity to sounds, lights, odors, tastes, or tactile sensations. Unable to filter out distracting sensations, and unable to integrate or reconcile the bombardment of sensory input, the autist copes through aversion and avoidance. He may also have areas of under-sensitivity—circumstances and settings in which he simply does not notice or become aware of sensory distinctions that would be obvious to most others in his position. In some cases, the autist may simply experience unusual or uncommon responses to sensory input, such as synesthesia.[53]

Davis Orientation provides a mechanism by which the individual can integrate and harmonize the sensory input, as well as a tool to foster consistency and accuracy of perceptions. By the time the client is working on the second construction, it is likely that his perceptual world has shifted to one of maintaining orientation for a substantial part of his waking hours. But the orientation tools cannot undo history, and there may be perceptual gaps or areas of confusion that are discovered and addressed in the course of the modeling or environmental explorations.

For example, Davis Facilitator Elizabeth Shier uncovered a significant hearing inaccuracy with a client, Michael, despite having previously worked with him using auditory orientation daily. She explains:

---

[53] Synesthesia is a mixing and blending of sensory impressions, such as seeing colors in association with certain musical notes. Daniel Tammet, a high-functioning autistic savant and author of the memoir, *Born on a Blue Day*, associated days of the week with specific colors, and numbers and words with specific shapes and patterns. (Tammet 2007) His synesthesia contributed to his prodigious memory and mathematics ability. He set a record by reciting the numbers of *pi* from memory to more than 20,000 digits; he also has an amazing facility to absorb new languages, which he attributes to being able to remember the shapes of new words. It has been reported that 15% of synesthetes have a first degree family history of autism, dyslexia or ADHD. (Cytowic 1995)

"We were doing environmental explorations in the kitchen. I had warmed up some lemon juice because Michael wanted to know if it was more sour if it was warm (it was!). I asked him what noise the microwave made. I was very surprised when he said, 'buzz.' It had actually made a 'beep, beep' sound. That led us to the piano to play a simple copying game. At first, Michael was completely unable to recreate even a two note pattern, but, with lots of laughing, he got it. This has greatly improved his listening skills at home too."

Another client chose to model the full body of an alligator as his first representation of *perception*. In his thought bubble, he created a model depicting only the alligator's head, with its huge mouth gaping open and filled with long sharp teeth. After an extended discourse, Facilitator Marcia Maust led him to discover that when oriented, the content of the thought bubble should match the real world object. All at once he smiled and said, "I get it! This is why, for my whole life, everyone always told me that I didn't see things the way they did!"[54]

Elizabeth Shier had a similar conversation with a little

---

[54] Lack of understanding of the idea that perception should match reality may also explain the difficulty autistic children typically have with false-belief tests. (Wellman, Cross and Watson 2001) (Baron-Cohen 1992) Typically, false-belief tests are used to assess "theory of mind," through the test subject's ability to extrapolate the mental belief of someone who has been deceived. Researchers assume that passing the test requires an understanding that a third person can have thoughts that diverge from reality and which differ from the knowledge possessed by the test subject. But it is also possible that some individuals provide the wrong answer on the test because of a core misunderstanding of their own thought processes, and of the difference between thought and reality,

girl who made a model of two little mice sitting up, with two little mice lying down resting in her thought bubble. With effort, the child realized that both parts had to match. In the past, the child had described so many situations from her school day inaccurately that the school no longer allowed her to be in a setting with only one teacher in the room. After her program, her mother reported a change in behavior. The child was no longer imprecise or bewildered when discussing past events because her perceptions had become grounded in reality.

Facilitator Alma Holden shares another example. When outdoors exploring the environment, she tripped over a branch on the ground. Her twelve-year-old client laughed, and then asked, "Is your perception good?" That opened the door to a discussion sorting out the idea of correct or incorrect perceptions, and relating those ideas to consequence, cementing the concept. The idea that internal perceptions are a mirror of the external, real world can be profound to an individual who has spent much of his life engulfed in a sense of chaos.

Thought—mental activity

The next basic concept is *thought,* defined as "mental activity." At this point the client is revisiting an idea that has been suggested previously with the modeling of *mind* as an aspect of *self,* where the concept of a clay bubble to represent thoughts was first introduced. The definition given for "mind" was "thought process," and both the phrase and the initial model incorporated the idea of "thought," using bits of clay placed within the bubble to depict a set of thoughts.

The clay thought bubble was reintroduced with the model of perception—so again, the client has previously created and understood a clay representation of mental activity. Thus, the thought model should be easy; through dialogue, the facilitator will guide the client to recognize that "thought" refers to the object inside the bubble for the simplest form model of perception.

However, at this stage a deeper understanding is added during the environmental explorations. The facilitator will introduce the idea of purposeful thought —thought that has a bearing on the external world. This idea grows from the concept of "thought" as a mere reflection of perception, but will lead to the concept of "thought" as a process of learning— of gaining knowledge, wisdom, and understanding about the external world and one's place within it. While the word "thought" can also refer to imaginative or free flowing thought—the stuff of daydreams—the concept is now explored as the precursor to a set of advanced concepts which encompass all forms of learning.

The facilitator gently guides the client to recognize "thought" as a vehicle of questioning and hypothesizing, through playing games such as having the client observe things and saying what he thinks. The facilitator might begin the game by saying something like, "I saw a child pick up a ball—I think he is going to throw it." The client is encouraged to make his own observations and offer his own ideas. Whereas the perception model depicted only passive thoughts resulting from mere observation, the facilitator now directs the client toward active mental activity. Whereas "thought" could once have been used to label the internal mental world of autism, the client now can see "thought"—the activity of his own mind—as an instrument for gaining insight and comprehending the external world.

The thought games chosen by the facilitator also reinforce the concepts from the first construction of *consequence, before and after, cause and effect.* To observe and speculate about what is going to happen next—or perhaps what has happened previously—is to bring the rules that govern the external world into the internal, mental world. In this way, the *thought* model and exercises help to integrate the two realms of the physical and mental world. The client is learning to think in a linear and logical fashion.

Experience—survive as changed

The third basic concept to be modeled is *experience*, which draws together the two concepts previously modeled (*perception* and *thought*). This model also links the second construction and the first,  connecting the concepts flowing from the root *change* with those derived from *continue.*

When the client has mastered the concepts of *perception* and *thought*, the next concept flows naturally: *experience* is what has happened to *self* as a result of self having a perception which registered as a thought. The *change* is whatever results from that thought process; at the simplest level, *self* now has a memory of a past event. Depending on the nature of the thought, *self* may change in other ways. For example, after tasting a new flavor of ice cream, *self* may have a changed opinion as to which type of ice cream he likes best.

The simplest form model can simply depict *self* along a time continuum, retaining the thought after the perceptual stimulus has passed. The facilitator will guide the client and reinforce the concept by engaging in activities which create experiences, and then having the client describe each experience.

The facilitator then moves on to explore the three different types of experience: in the role of an observer, at the point of cause, or the point of effect. These three roles were introduced at the outset of the modeling of the first construction, as part of the process of mastery. So the task at this point is to provide the client with a name for each of these types of experience. These are the three concepts that Davis has chosen to label *understanding* (from observation), *knowledge* (from experiencing effect), and *wisdom* (from being the cause).

Because these three concepts represent different aspects of the broader concept, *experience*, the facilitator and client can work with the already created model, simply using discussion to clearly identify what is going on in the model, making minor adjustments, and using dominant arrows as needed to indicate which word relates to which aspect of the model.

understanding: experience of observing

(*self* is in the center, observing the ball)

knowledge: experience of being at effect

(the ball bumps into *self*)

wisdom: experience of being at cause

(*self* has influenced the position of the ball)

Of course, the clay modeling is again supplemented with activities and explorations that reinforce and draw the client's attention to each type of experience. Every possible experience will fit into at least one of these categories—thus there is no limit on what activities the facilitator and client may undertake together.

The words used—experience, understanding, knowledge, wisdom—are not new. They were an integral part of the recitation used to identify the clay model of *self*: *"You represent me. You represent every experience 'me' has ever had, all of the knowledge, all of the wisdom, and all of the understanding."* With the mastery of these concepts, the client is now able to fully comprehend the meaning of those words, to appreciate that "me" is comprised of experience built of knowledge, wisdom and understanding. In that way, the concepts learned will become integrated into the client's identity.

The second construction is now complete.

Chapter 9

The Third Construction:
The Importance of Emotion

The third construction is built on the root concept *energy*, and provides an in-depth exploration of *lifeforce,* the third aspect of *self.* It provides the means by which the first two constructions, built on the concepts of *change* and *continue*, are brought together to give the client a growing sense of purpose in his life. It differs from the other constructions in that rather than being built on readily observable states of the physical world—ideas like *change* and *continue*—it stems from a more abstract concept, and moves to an exploration of the internal world of *feelings.* This exploration is essential to provide the client with a sense of wholeness, but the series of concepts explored may be less intuitive to the outside observer or helper. The concepts are labeled with ordinary and common words, but the definitions supplied are specific to the task and goals of the construction.

The Foundations of Emotion

Within the third construction, "emotion" is the first of four basic concepts to be explored. That is, it lies on the third step up the pyramid of root, base, and basic concepts, and rests upon knowledge gained from the experience of a root concept.

The word *emotion* comes from the Latin root word for movement; literally, it means, "to move out." Davis defines *emotion* as "self created energy"—that is, the impetus within self that leads to movement. With this definition, the concept of emotion becomes a bridge to the other basic concepts—*want, need,* and *intention*—which are the inner feelings that drive human beings to action. Those are concepts that the autistic individual needs to recognize and master both for the sake of his own individual development, and as a foundation for anticipating and comprehending the behavior of others.

Despite the derivation of the word, most dictionaries define "emotion" in terms of feeling, such as "any of the feelings of joy, sorrow, fear, hate, love, etc."[55] But that definition is merely descriptive—it does not lead to an understanding of the source of emotion, or the value that emotions play in our lives and being.

Facilitator Gabriela Scholter shares this story about a young man I'll call Kurt: "I just met a boy, 15 years old, best in his class in every single subject including sports, and quite autistic. He can speak, if he wants to, but his perpetual question is, '*And what is that good for?*' Whether it is going outside, baking a cake or whatever—if it isn't

---

[55]   emotion. Dictionary.com. Dictionary.com Unabridged. Random House, Inc.   http://dictionary.reference.com/browse/emotion (accessed: September 23, 2011).

school-related he needs to know what it's good for. It is as though the only thing in his life that makes any sense is school." One assumes that the young man would not be satisfied if the answer to his question was merely, "This is fun" or "It gives us enjoyment."

Ray Davis worked with a nine-year-old boy who was quite an expert on everything to do with various makes and models of cars. After modeling the concept of *change*, Ray was walking outdoors with young Brandon exploring the environment, when suddenly the boy started to laugh—a deep, hearty belly laugh. Ray asked what was so funny. Barely able to contain his laughter, Brandon pointed to a car and stammered, "Honda wheels on a Toyota!"

Ray laughed too, and then asked Brandon which type of car was his favorite. The boy could not answer—he just stared at Ray with a puzzled look. The boy's intellect had allowed him to spot a set of mismatched hubcaps in an instant, and he was fully capable of feeling a sense of amusement, expressed through his laughter. But he had not integrated the idea that his emotions could give rise to an opinion—he could not use his own emotions to guide his choices and actions.

Both Brandon and Kurt were able to use their intellect to learn about subjects that interested them. They also were internally driven by the positive feelings they associated with their respective interests and achieve-ments, but they did not see or understand those interests as being driven by their internal emotions. Instead, it is likely that they saw their interests as being driven by external factors of real-world importance. Brandon thought cars were objectively important; Kurt placed similar value on his performance at school and athletics.

To achieve the goals of the autism program, the client must learn that "emotion" is an internal, driving force.

Humans choose to engage in activities in furtherance of their wants, and their wants are driven by internal emotions. We want what makes us happy, or what supports our personal, long term goals. The autistic client needs to understand that the internal want is driven by emotion.

While it is quite possible that a person may be able to offer detailed rational explanations as to why he is acting in a certain way, his actual performance is ultimately driven by emotions. Merely knowing that something is important or valuable is not enough if one's heart is not in the task.

Because Davis defines "emotion" as "self created energy," there must be an understanding of the root concept "energy." That is why *energy*—something unseen that exists in nature—is the third root concept to be mastered.

And because "emotion" does in fact derive from naturally occurring internal feelings, it is important to explore the genesis of those feelings. This is done at the outset by modeling the concept of *urge*. The order for the third construction is to first model *urge,* then *energy,* then *force*, all as preparation for the basic concept, *emotion.*

Urge—The Instinctual Desire to Seek Pleasure and Avoid Pain

The third construction begins with a model of the concept of *urge. Urge* is not a root concept, but rather the underpinning of the concepts to be explored. The root concepts are laws of nature, ideas that represent constants in the external world. Because the concepts are labels for conditions that occur without being seen or sensed, an autistic person usually has little understanding of them until the root concept is explored with the facilitator.

An *urge,* on the other hand, is an internal feeling that the client will be very familiar with, though he might not have given it a name, or thought to relate one type of urge to another. The urge is part of our genetic programming— it is the inner drive that is essential to the survival of any creature, as it is what drives us to seek nourishment and shelter, and try to avoid physical harm.

Urges provide the energy that drive our survival and also enable us to experience emotions. The *urge* is the starting point of the *lifeforce.*

Because *urge* does not represent a new discovery to the autistic client, but rather a name that defines a familiar part of his internal experience, the modeling process is relatively fast. The facilitator will discuss the  idea with the client and guide the construction of a model.

There are two new additions to the clay language introduced with this model: the feeling bubble, and the miniature self model. The feeling bubble is used to represent something happening within *self:* the *feeling* that accompanies the image that is modeled. The end of the clay loop is attached to the chest of the *self* model, rather than its head, to signify that it represents a feeling, or emotion, rather than a thought.

As the client proceeds through the third construction and advanced concepts, his models will end up containing a growing number of small *self* models. These represent the self contained within thoughts and feelings. The smaller size helps to distinguish the parts of the model that are "physically real" from the parts that are thought or felt. Also, as a practical matter, as the models get more complex, it is easier to manage if the additional pieces of the model are kept as small as reasonably possible.

Like other simplest form models, the *urge* model relies on simple clay balls used to represent a larger idea. In the *urge* model, a clay ball at the foot of a small self can represent "pain" (wanting, but not having, the ball); and a clay ball in the hands of a second small self can represent "pleasure" (having the desired ball in hand). An arrow from the "pain" to the "pleasure" scenario demonstrates that *urge* is the desire to seek the pleasurable experience.

The Root Concept: Energy (Potential to Influence)

The third root concept is *energy*, which Davis describes as "potential to influence." This is a sophisticated definition of the term, perhaps one that stems from Davis' own background in engineering. Most dictionaries or school texts define "energy" in terms of the result of its influence—for example, as something that generates heat (thermal) or drives physical activity (mechanical). But those definitions are drawn from the effect of energy, not energy itself, and the definitions would vary depending on context. A *root* concept is simple, drawn from nature—its definition must be equally simple and applicable to energy in all its forms.

Engineer David Watson explains energy as "the ability to make something happen", which is very close to the Davis definition.[56] Since energy exists whether or not it is

---

[56] David Watson is the creator of the educational web site, FT Exploring Science and Technology. The definition above appears at *(continued on next page)*

invoked or realized, Davis defines it as a "potential."[57] In any form, energy has the potential to instigate change—that is what is meant by the words "to influence." Because of that potential, energy supplies a linkage between the other root concepts, "change" and "continue." In other words, in order for there to be "change," there must also be energy.

A person cannot see, feel, or observe energy itself; the person can only observe the change that results from the release or transformation of energy. A Davis Facilitator can explain the concept to a client with a simple demonstration of kinetic energy, by holding a clay ball above a table and then dropping it. Of course the clay ball will land on the table with a thud, and the round ball will become somewhat flattened when it lands. *Energy* is what was in the ball before it landed—while it was still airborne and moving. When the ball hit the table, the energy was converted to *force*—but up until the moment when the moving ball comes in contact with an unyielding object (the table), the *energy* remained invisible. In this context, *energy* is not the movement of the ball (something that can be seen), but the power within the falling ball to create a

---

(continued from previous page)

http://www.ftexploring.com/energy/definition.html (retrieved September 20, 2011). An alternative statement, "Energy is that 'certain something' inside stuff ... that makes everything happen," is offered at http://www.ftexploring.com/energy/energy-1.htm (retrieved September 20, 2011)

[57] The Davis use of the word "potential" is not the same as the scientific term, "potential energy," as used to distinguish the energy in a stationary object from "kinetic energy." Rather, Davis uses the word "potential" in its ordinary sense, to reflect the possibility that something might not occur. Davis does not use the word "ability" in the energy definition, because the word "ability" is given its own special meaning as a fourth level concept.

loud noise and change its shape when coming in contact with the table. That power was created within the ball itself as a consequence of the movement—but its effect was a mere potential within the ball until the moment of impact with the table.

After modeling the concept in clay, the idea of energy can be explored in the environment by setting objects in motion: kicking a ball, rolling a marble, turning on a tap. This is only one type of energy—kinetic energy, which is the energy generated as a consequence of movement—but it suffices for purposes of mastering the concept.[58] This part of the Davis program would be a good beginning for the study of physics, but that is not the goal of Identity Development. In this context, *energy* needs to be understood only to the extent that it applies to human behavior.

The Base Concept: Force (Application of Energy)

The base concept for *energy* is *force*, which Davis defines simply as the "application of energy." A base concept is one that expresses the way we, as humans, experience the unseen root concept. In the case of energy, the base is so closely tied to the root that it is hard to mentally

---

[58] In physics, energy can be categorized as either existing within an object in motion (kinetic) or existing within an object at rest (potential). Energy can also be categorized by the way the energy is expressed (chemical, mechanical, electrical, thermal, etc.). These differences are not relevant to understanding the root concept. Davis' use of kinetic energy in the model and environmental explorations is simply the example of energy that is easiest to demonstrate and depict.

separate the two. That is why the demonstration of energy with a falling ball needed to also include a demonstration of force, as the effect of the ball striking the table.

In other words, it was necessary to include the idea of force in order to explain what energy does. F*orce* is the result of energy being transformed. In the case of our model of kinetic energy, the transformation occurs upon impact with another object. The clay model of *force* will need to show the impact and resultant change. Because the goal is identity development, this will be modeled with *self* at the point of impact, with a model of a rolling ball striking self. Without the *self*-involved model, there would be the risk that the autistic client would get the idea of *force* but fail to integrate it within his identity. In this case, *self* is put at the effect point in order to lay the foundation for the next concepts to be modeled, which relate to how *self* responds to internally created energy.

The modeling of *force* also ties the energy series to the original idea of *lifeforce.* While that concept might have been first understood to stem from something unexplained or magical, with the energy/force models, *lifeforce* becomes a concept that follows its own set of natural rules. That is, *lifeforce* is the way that life-energy is expressed. As the word *lifeforce* was defined as being tied to an *urge,* this also links the concept of an *urge* to energy and to emotion.

The environmental explorations for *force* can be fun, as the facilitator can guide the client to use and apply *force* in different contexts, such as toppling over a tower of blocks, triggering a chain reaction of falling dominoes, or throwing a ball against a wall. The point of the exercises is to be able to identify the points of impact where energy is converted to force.

The Basic Concepts: Emotion, Want, Need, Intention

The third construction is completed with the modeling of four concepts, which together provide meaning for the final sentence of the script associated with the model of *self:* "You represent ... my urge to be who and what I am." Basic concepts are the ideas reflecting knowledge that is derived from the experience of the root concept. The third root concept is *energy,* but the modeling began with the concept of *urge,* because the construction is focused on how human *energy* combined with *urge* is transformed into action and behavior.

The four basic concepts derived from *energy* are closely related, and can be built upon the same model, extended as needed with the addition of new elements.

Emotion—self created energy

The goal of Davis Concept Mastery is to introduce and explore a series of *concepts* or abstract ideas, not to learn a set of dictionary definitions. In many cases, the Davis definition of a concept aligns closely with the dictionary definition, but for some concepts a word has to be selected to match an idea that is not easily represented by a single word. Davis has chosen to correlate ordinary words with the new ideas, rather than try to invent new words to fit. *Emotion* is one of those concept words.

For purposes of the autism program, Davis defines emotion as *self created energy.* This does not mean that Davis is ignoring or repudiating the ordinary sense of the word, as representing a feeling such as joy or sorrow.[59]

---

[59] Dictionary.com provide the following definition of emotion: "an affective state of consciousness in which joy, sorrow, fear, hate, or the like, is experienced, as distinguished from cognitive and volitional states of consciousness." Dictionary.com Unabridged.

(continued on next page)

Rather, Davis is incorporating that sense and at the same time going beyond that definition, to elucidate the psychological and physiological function that emotions serve. Davis is answering the question that the 15-year-old Kurt asked with each new activity: *What is that good for?*

One pervasive characteristic of autism is a difference in the way emotions are processed and understood. Autists experience a full range of emotions, but the triggers and level of intensity of specific feelings differ from the common responses of neurotypical individuals. That difference underlies the sense of isolation and difficulty with social relationships that are part of the autistic experience.

Unfortunately, the autist may be most aware of negative emotions, such as the overpowering sense of rage or fear that triggers a meltdown. The author Eric Chen listed the following emotions as part of his experience growing up: *confusion, shock, despair, frustration, resentment, loneliness, depression.*[60] An autist's feelings of positive emotions, such as contentment or gratification, may be associated with activities, habits or possessions that are viewed with disapproval by society at large, such as hand-flapping or other autistic mannerisms. Lorna's client Max carried a plastic fork and a wooden skewer wherever he went—it gave him a sense of comfort to wave those objects around in his hands. But his self-comforting habit probably caused the opposite effect in neurotypical observers, who may have felt disconcerted at the sight of a young child brandishing sharp objects.

Given this mismatch between internal feelings and the

(continued from previous page)

Random House, Inc.   http://dictionary.reference.com/browse/emotion (accessed: September 23, 2011).

[60] (E. Y. Chen 2007, 125-127)

task of adapting to the world at large, it would be natural for the autist to try to repress or ignore his emotions, even if he were not also plagued with the unstable orientation and incomplete individuation that gave rise to the autism in the first place. Of course, it is more likely that the autist simply has little conscious awareness of his emotions and their impact on him. He feels, but he has not perceived his feeling to be separate and apart from whatever activity is associated with that feeling, or has not ascribed a causal relation between feeling and event. Given this background, within the context of a Davis program, it would serve no useful purpose to explore the idea of emotions using traditional definitions. The autist may have yet to explore and discover a world in which feelings such as joy or sorrow are helpful to him.

But emotions serve a very real, and very necessary, purpose closely related to survival. The internalized sensation that humans associate with specific emotions come from chemicals naturally produced by the body, precisely as a way to regulate behavior. An obvious example is the action of the amygdala, the brain's rapid response center. When exposed to a fear-producing stimulus—for example, a venomous snake—the amygdala springs into action even before the person becomes consciously aware of the fearsome object, triggering the release of adrenaline and other excitatory hormones into the bloodstream. Those hormones in turn prime the body for action—the heart rate increases, hearing and vision become more acute, the person breaks into a sweat.

At the other extreme, the hormone oxytocin primes the body for love and tenderness. Easily triggered by the sight of a newborn infant, the oxytocin-saturated brain is more trusting and affectionate, as well as being less vigilant.[61] Survival requires that individuals protect themselves from danger, but it also requires that parents nurture rather than attack or flee their children, so a different chemically-modulated response is needed.

On a biological level, emotions represent the sensation that humans associate with different balances of chemicals in their brain and bloodstream. Serotonin is sometimes called "the happy hormone;" the hormone anandanine draws its name from the Sanskrit word for "bliss;" testosterone is often associated with anger and belligerence; dopamine is associated with a sense of pleasure, excitement, and reward. Mood-altering drugs and medications that are commonly prescribed to treat anxiety or depression work by influencing the action of brain receptors already specialized to specific naturally-occurring chemicals. The drugs either act as substitute chemicals and bind to those same receptors, or affect the rate at which the natural chemicals are produced or reabsorbed in the brain. Dr. Candace Pert, the pharmacologist who discovered the brain's opiate receptor, explained, "Emotions are neuropeptides attaching to receptors and stimulating an electrical charge on neurons."[62]

---

[61] Autism may be associated with inborn differences in the way the brain responds to oxytocin. Multiple studies suggest an association between autism and variations in the oxytocin receptor gene (OXTR). (Lerer, et al. 2008) (Jacob, et al. 2007) Autistic adults who received oxytocin in an experimental setting showed improvement in their ability to recognize the emotional significance of speech intonation. (Hollander, et al. 2007)

[62] A "peptide" is a chemical compound consisting of a chain of two or more amino acids. Dictionary.com. *The American Heritage® Science Dictionary.* Houghton Mifflin Company: http://dictionary .reference.com/browse/peptide (accessed: September 21, 2011).

(continued on next page)

Davis' functional and psychological definition of emotion mirrors the biological process—it is a form of energy with the potential to stimulate a change of state in neurons. At the biological level, the energy precedes the sensation—that is, the energy is contained within the chemical that was produced by the body in response to some stimuli. That is also how Davis sees the process, by defining "emotion" as the energy itself, as opposed to defining emotion in terms of the feelings produced.

The core principle is that emotions drive human response and action. At the level of an urge, the interactions of brain chemicals are necessary for the survival of the species. They spur newborns to suckle and seek nourishment, they trigger older children and adults to take action to protect themselves from physical harm, and they provide the blood/brain chemistry that fosters reproduction and child-rearing.

But emotions are more than urges; they are the product of urge plus life experience. Over time, an individual learns to associate the chemically-induced feelings with a wide variety of life events. The brain/body connection means that humans are capable of triggering the production of various brain chemicals through their thought process and memories. When a person thinks about a time that he learned good news and felt happy, the happy memory will trigger the body to produce the chemicals that bring back a sense of the happy emotions. If the person ruminates over events that made him sad or

---

(continued from previous page)

A "neuropeptide" is a molecule that influences neural activity or functioning. Dictionary.com. *Merriam-Webster's Medical Dictionary*. Merriam-Webster, Inc.: http://dictionary.reference.com/browse/neuropeptide (accessed: September 21, 2011). Candace Pert is the author of the book, *Molecules of Emotion*. (Pert 1999)

angry, he similarly will experience a resurgence of the negative emotions associated with that event. People regularly habituate themselves to associate certain activities and events with certain emotions—and that in turn drives their behavior. Perhaps an adult drags herself out of bed to go to work out at the gym; after she exercises, she feels relaxed and happy. The next day she repeats the same routine. Soon, after successive days of happiness at the gym, she is waking up happy and eager to go—she doesn't have to wait until the end of her exercise regimen to feel good. Instead the happy thoughts and feelings come with the very thought of going to the gym, and, in turn, become the motivating factor that keeps her going day after day.[63]

Davis defines *emotion* as "self created energy" precisely because of this internal power each person has to regulate and drive their own emotions, whether or not the person is consciously aware of the connection. At the level of *urge*, the feeling is simply triggered by *perception* (external awareness). The feeling is intense, and in the moment.

An *urge* itself is simple and primitive, the type of sensation that humans share with animals, most closely tied to survival. But the sophistication of human thought

---

[63] This type of habituation is the foundation of behavioral training based on positive or negative reinforcement. When a person (or animal) is given a reward, the experience of pleasure coincides with a burst of dopamine production in the brain. With repetition, the person comes to associate the reward-inducing behavior with pleasure, and the brain begins to produce dopamine in anticipation of the behavior, just as Pavlov's dogs salivated on hearing the bell they associated with their meals. Behavioral training relies on that hormonal, emotion-producing rush to shape future behavior. Unfortunately, that is also the same mechanism that fuels many addictions, such as compulsive gambling.

and consciousness is tied to a far more complicated array of emotions.[64]

A memory is the brain's reconstruction of a perception. In essence, it is a mental image that has been retained from a past experience—or it could be the recollection of a sound, a tactile sensation, a flavor, an odor. Davis Concept Mastery focuses on mental pictures, as they support scenarios that can be easily modeled in clay, and also because it is likely that most of our memories with emotional resonance are tied to some sort of mental image. That is, when a person hears the strains of a cherished piece of music, it is likely that the sounds also bring a mental picture associated with the music. When a person remembers the taste of chocolate, his mind might also conjure up a picture of a fudge brownie.

Every memory also has an associated feeling, which is the feeling that was experienced at the time the memory was made. This is inherent in the structure of the brain and the way memories are stored. Emotions are driven by the limbic system of the brain, which includes the brain structures primarily involved in regulating and producing the various hormones. Memory is strongly influenced by the hippocampus and amygdala. Long-term memories of events or experiences are preserved through action of the hippocampus. Damage or destruction of the hippocampus will impair the ability to form new long-term memories. The intensity of the memory is influenced by stress hormones produced by the amygdala; the greater the state of emotional arousal at the time the memory is formed, the more intense and persistent the memory.

---

[64] At the biological level, scientists have now identified roughly 60 different chemical neurotransmitters. When produced in combination and at varying levels of intensity, there are endless possibilities for emotional resonance.

Thus, the emotional, hormone-signaling center of the brain is crucial to forming memories. Without emotion, we would probably have little or no long-term memory of past events.[65]

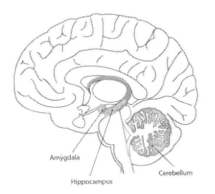

From a psychological perspective, we can consider that memories of past events are a way of reviving the feelings that went along with the past event. The person doing the remembering exists only in the present, but when he conjures up a mental picture from the past, he is transferring the past *feeling* into his present awareness. Because that represents a *change* in his present state—he *feels* differently inside—there must be some type of *energy* accompanying the change. Davis uses the word "emotion" to describe the energy that has the power to alter feelings. As this is something that is created by *self* in the process of resurrecting a previously stored memory, the definition given to *emotion* is *self-created energy*.

The clay model of emotion is more complex than previous models. To depict all of the ideas from the definition, the model requires a representation of the following concepts: self; some tangible object associated with pleasure, in the form of an object that self would like to have; a thought bubble representing a mental picture of

---

[65] The hippocampus is essential for the formation and preservation of *episodic* memory, but not *procedural* memory. So a person who has lost function of the hippocampus would not be able to remember experiences or events, but might still remember learned skills, such as how to drive a car or play the piano. Procedural memory is tied to the cerebellum and motor areas of the brain.

self seeing but not having the desired object; a separate thought bubble containing the imagined self in possession of the desired object; and an arrow connecting the two thoughts, representing the shifting of mental attention toward the image representing attainment of the desired object. There must also be a representation of the feeling that accompanies the two thoughts: two self models, with and without the desired object, contained within a feeling bubble. The model will also include a depiction of the energy that occurs in tandem with the change of state, using an arrow within the feeling bubble which points to the self model with the desired object.

This view of *emotion* is a profound concept, and it is likely that a Davis Facilitator will spend extra time with her client exploring the idea. With the environmental explorations, the facilitator will be creating opportunities to engage with other people, encouraging the client to look at their faces and attend to their tone of voice, and then later prompting the client to venture a guess as to how the other person might have been feeling. Perhaps the client will present a small gift, such as a flower, to a sibling. How did the sibling respond? Did she smile? Did her tone of voice change? Did she feel happy? Surprised?

Of course these exercises do more than simply draw the client's attention to the creation and existence of an emotion. By linking the emotion to actions and events, and encouraging the client to pay attention to faces and facial expressions, and changes in vocal intonations, the facilitator is nurturing the foundational social skills that generally are difficult for autistic individuals. In the context of understanding *emotion*, the client is also learning to focus his own attention more on the emotion-generating aspects of his interactions with others.

Human social interaction is driven primarily by emotion, not reason. Because autistic individuals do not experience and respond to emotional impulses in the same way as others around them, their social skills are hampered. As the autist becomes more high functioning, he may try to use reason to explain and anticipate the behavior of other people, and of course he fails—he doesn't recognize that people behave irrationally when they are joking or playful, or when they are feeling angry or hurt.

When emotions are understood as *self-created energy*, they are imbued with a new power. At one level the client becomes more self-empowered, because he will gain the ability to recognize, harness and redirect his own emotions to make his life more meaningful and rewarding. As the client becomes more comfortable and familiar with the emotions that reside within himself, he also gains insight into the emotions of others. He will develop the ability to first ask, and later intuit, what another person may be feeling in response to his statements and actions, and to reciprocate in ways that foster the development of social relationships.

Davis Facilitator Cinda Osterman shares this account of working with a 12-year old boy who had always been very reluctant to speak to strangers:

"Joel enjoyed every concept he modeled, but especially emotion. When he came back from our observations, he was so excited. He really enjoyed seeing how people changed when given a compliment. The same evening, he went out to dinner with his parents at a nice restaurant. His mother was stunned at what happened: Joel liked his meal so much that he asked the waitress if he could thank the chef personally. She was very impressed and immediately fetched the chef. Looking directly at him, Joel told the chef how much he liked his entrée and especially the special dessert. The chef obviously was very pleased. Later, Joel told his mother that he felt ready to take on the world and can't wait to start finding new challenges."

Want—urge to exist as

The next basic concept is *want*, defined simply as "urge to exist as." This definition is framed so as to build upon and relate to the other Davis concepts, as well as to relate the concept to the Identity Development process.

The word *urge* in the definition reinforces an understanding that the source of *want* is the instinctual drive to seek pleasure and avoid pain. The phrase "to exist" relates the concept of *want* back to the second construction, of "continue" and "survive"—*existence* is synonymous with survival. The addition of the word "as" to the definition suggests change: a *want* represents an internal urge to create a change that benefits the individual's survival. This is what forms the *lifeforce* "urge to be who and what I am."

Again, the Davis definition is geared to enabling the autistic client to relate the idea explored to his conception of self, and to fostering the process of inner growth and development. It is also framed as a building block for the concepts that follow.

The process of modeling the concept is quite easy. The elements of the *want* model are exactly the same as the *emotion* model—self; a desired object; two separate mental images in thought bubbles representing the state of not having, and of having, the desired object; and a feeling bubble encompassing both images, with an arrow representing the transition in the direction of the small self holding the desired object.

The only thing that changes in the *want* model is that the dominant arrow points to the small self in the feeling bubble holding the desired object, because a *want* is an emotion triggered by a mental image of *self* doing or having whatever it is that underlies the desire. So whereas *emotion* is the energy brought on by the image of the change in status (from not having to having), *want* is simply the part of the model where that energy is directed.

Explorations with the facilitator can simply involve pointing out things or events that the client might want, or might not want. Of course this provides practice in thinking about and expressing an emotion-driven opinion, building the ability for a boy like Brandon to be able to consider which model of car he likes best.

Need—something that satisfies want

Until the modeling of *need*, the third construction concepts are focused on internal feelings and thoughts. The concept of *need* links the internal thought/feeling world to the outside world. The *need* is a real-world object or action that satisfies the internal feeling that accompanies *want*.

If a person *wants* to eat ice-cream, that *want* is satisfied by going to a shop and purchasing an ice cream cone. If the person *wants* to play basketball, the *want* is satisfied by having a basketball in hand on a court. If the person *wants* to listen to music, the *want* is satisfied when the radio is turned on to a favorite station.

The clay model for emotion/ want requires only one more element: a representation of the real-world object of desire, something that *self* can observe which is outside his thoughts and feeling. This can be shown by placing a model of the desired object (a clay ball) in front of self, marked by a dominant arrow.

Because *need* is external to *self*, some sort of physical action is required for the *need* to be attained or achieved. In other words, *need* has two parts: the object itself, and the action or event that will result in the need being realized. Usually that is something that a person must initiate on his own, unless he is fortunate enough to have a family member or friend anticipate his *want* and independently fulfill the *need*. Parents are adept at being the independent actors who fill the *needs* of young children unbidden, but to meaningfully participate in life the client must develop the ability to act on his own initiative.

The action part is not shown in the model, but will be incorporated into the explorations with the facilitator. This prepares the client for the modeling of the concepts that follow *need* (*intention,* and the fourth level concepts of *motivation, ability,* and *control*). In explorations with the facilitator, the client will practice identifying wants and needs, both in himself and in others. Part of that process will be discussing or specifying what the person has to *do* in order to get the needed item. For example, if the client wants to eat a banana, he will have to go to the kitchen and get one; if his sister wants to play outside, she will have to open the back door. In this way, the facilitator is laying the groundwork for the next step.

Intention—urge to satisfy need

The final basic concept model of the third construction is *intention*. With this concept, the focus returns to an internalized feeling within *self*, and will be represented in clay with the addition of a feeling bubble to the existing model of *need*. The definition of *intention* is "urge to satisfy need." The difference between a *want* and an *intention* is that there must be an action that will cause the change of status that *need* represents. The model within the added feeling bubble will depict a small *self* taking the needed action—such as bending down to pick up the clay ball.

Because there is an action required to satisfy need, there is also a require-ment of energy. The amount of required energy corres-ponds to the contemplated action—the more difficult or complicated the task, the greater the energy needed. If the task is to be completed by *self*, then the source of the energy will be *emotion*. The difference between *want* and *intention* is a combination of the recognition of *need* and the intensity of the *emotion*. The more intense the emotion, the more energy produced. Intention is a mental picture or feeling that triggers an emotion of sufficient intensity to get the job done.

In other words, if a person wants a glass of milk but is feeling too tired to get out of his chair, he will not get up to go to the kitchen, open the refrigerator, and pour the milk into a glass, unless the emotional intensity of the *want* for milk is sufficient to overcome the competing emotion of wanting to continue to enjoy the comfort of the chair. Of course, in physics and in life, extra energy is required to overcome inertia. More energy is needed for a person sitting in a living room chair to get the milk than for a person already standing in front of the refrigerator to accomplish the same task.

This can be illustrated by going back to the model of kinetic energy from the clay ball dropping. In order to create the energy, the ball first has to be lifted from the table. If it is lifted only a few inches and dropped, there will not be much energy in the ball—it will land softly on the table and probably will hold its shape. But if the ball is lifted higher, and dropped from a distance of two feet, then it will make a much louder noise when it lands on the table, and the force of impact will cause one side of the ball to flatten to a much greater degree.

In environmental explorations, the facilitator will encourage her client to observe the actions and behavior of other people and speculate as to their intentions. For example, if a neighbor is seen walking toward her mailbox, she probably intends to pick up her mail; if a man is seen putting a leash on his dog's collar, perhaps he intends to take the dog for a walk.

As with other activities, these explorations not only reinforce the understanding of the concept modeled, but also provide an opportunity to put that knowledge into action by practicing a new life skill—in this case, the ability to use observation to anticipate the unspoken intentions of other people.

Chapter 10

Completing the Process:
Common and Advanced Concepts

After the completion of the three constructions, the client is ready to model a set of more sophisticated concepts that join and unite the three root constructions based on *change, continue,* and *energy.* The process of Identity Development will be complete when the separate constructions are brought together and put into action. The first three constructions were focused on exploring the different aspects of *body, mind,* and *lifeforce;* the final steps are geared to bringing those ideas together into a unitary *self.*

The final sequence of models and exploration gives the client the tools needed for self-actualization. Davis defines *lifeforce* as "the urge to be who and what 'I' am." The final four concepts to be modeled and the exercise that follows will give the client the ability to turn that urge into action.

The Common Concepts—Motivation, Ability, Control

During the first three constructions, the client modeled a series of concepts on three levels: root, base, and basic. For the next step of the program, there are three Common Concepts, or Fourth Level Concepts, to be mastered. Davis defines a Common Concept as one that is derived from at least two of the three root concepts.

Motivation—urge to control

The definitions of the three Common Concepts are overlapping; that is, each concept incorporates one of the other two concepts in its definition. That means that a full understanding can be reached only after all three are modeled. However, all three build upon the same clay model of *intention* that was on the table at the end of the third construction.

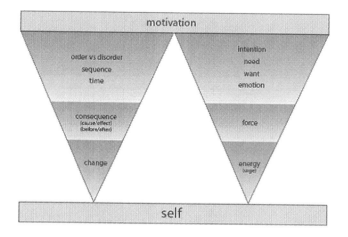

A Davis Facilitator will proceed in the order dictated by elements that need to be added to the clay model. She will start with the concept of *motivation,* because all the elements of the motivation model are already included with the model of *intention.* The only difference is that motivation is depicted by the entire model, rather than by any individual element. All that needs to be done is to build upon the existing knowledge and understanding.

Motivation is defined as "urge to control." *Control,* in turn, is defined as "ability to cause change," but the client will not model that concept until after modeling "ability."

However, the client understands the concept of causing change from the first construction; thus, the elements needed for the motivation model are already in place.

Motivation links the two constructions of change and energy—it is the product of a combination of the desire to cause change with the energy to do so. So *motivation* exists when there is a combination of the self-created energy with an awareness of actions needed to achieve a goal.

For the environmental explorations, the facilitator will encourage the client to observe the actions of the people they encounter, and to speculate on the intention which is the source of the motivation for the action they observe. For example, a woman is observed purchasing a sandwich at a café. The motivation to buy the sandwich is a product of the woman's intention to eat it. (To turn it around: if the woman intends to eat a sandwich, then the action required to realize that intention is that she must first buy the desired item.)

Ability—knowledge, skill and opportunity to Control

The next Common Concept explored is *ability,* which links the *change* and *continue* roots. The *change* root provided an understanding of cause and effect, consequence, time, sequence, and order vs. disorder. The *continue* root explored the ideas of thought and perception, and culminated with *experience.*

Ability is defined by Davis as "knowledge, skill and opportunity to control." "Control" is the "ability to cause change." So the idea of "control" stems directly from the *change* root—it is simply a matter of putting *self* at the cause point of change.

"Knowledge, skill and opportunity" are all ideas that draw on the *continue* root. The concept of *knowledge* ("experience of being at effect") has already been modeled, but needs to be incorporated into the model of *ability.*

Davis defines *skill* as "experienced in causing a desired change." In other words, *skill* is something gained as a result of practice of being at *cause*, a base concept within the *change* root. Within the *ability* model, the *knowledge* needed is that which is gained from *skill*. That knowledge is gained from the experience of being at the point of *effect* of the self-initiated change.

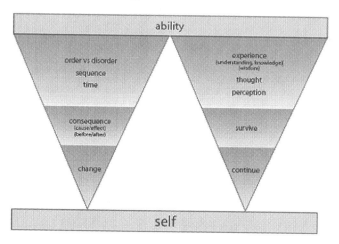

For example, if we move beyond the task of merely picking up a ball at rest and instead consider the *knowledge* required to catch a ball that has been tossed or struck by a bat, we can see that the experienced baseball player needs more than simply skill at catching balls. He also needs to know which of multiple ball-catching skills is needed to catch that particular ball. Does he leap high into the air to intercept the ball? Can he stand in place and reach out as the ball comes to him? Or does he need to run back across the field, judging the trajectory of a high flying ball, so that he can be properly positioned in the right spot, at the right time, to grab and hold onto the ball as it falls to earth? He gained his *skill* at catching balls through hours of practice with many different balls; he gained his knowledge from experiencing the consequence of the choices he made during practice. For example, he knows from past mistakes that if he uses the wrong ball-catching technique, it is possible that he will catch the ball only to have it bounce from his glove onto the ground.

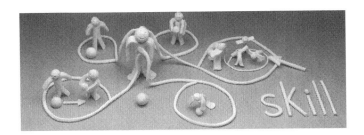

For the *ability* model to incorporate the ideas of *knowledge* and *skill*, two new elements must be added to the *motivation* model: a depiction of *self* gaining a skill through practice, and a depiction of *self* in possession of the knowledge gained through the exercise of *skill*. That can be done with a thought bubble within a thought bubble. The main, large *self* at the center of the model is given an additional thought bubble; in addition to the first two thought bubbles with mental images of the two states of not having, and having, the ball, there will be added a thought bubble that represents the *knowledge* needed to get the ball. Within the third thought bubble, there is a smaller *self* who is imbued with that knowledge.

Because the small *self* gained his knowledge through the attainment of a *skill*, that model has its own smaller thought bubble, and in that bubble a depiction of skill: at least three very small *selfs* engaged in the skill-building activity of bending down to pick up the ball. The clay elements are the same for both models; the only difference will be the placement of the dominant arrows signifying *knowledge* or *skill*.

The third element of *ability* is "opportunity to control." A person cannot use and apply knowledge and skill without the opportunity. In other words, our hypothetical baseball player cannot catch a ball unless one first comes his way.

Davis defines *opportunity* as "authority, time, place and conditions to act." There is no need to build clay models of each separate word encompassed in that definition, but the facilitator will spend several hours with the client exploring the ideas through dialogue, and observing and discussing examples found in the environment.

Teachers who read this book will be very familiar with the problem of lack of authority as being an impediment to action—they often have a very clear idea of how to apply their knowledge and skills to a situation, but are prevented from doing so because their ideas run counter to a newly adopted curriculum, or do not fit within the allotted time schedule.

For our imagined baseball player, the authority may come from the rules of the game. If he is on second base, he will not attempt to catch a ball that is flying toward the player in the short stop position, even if he suspects that his teammate is about to flub the catch.

In our simplest form clay model, the authority is generated within *self*. In this case, self had *authority* because he did not need anyone's permission to touch the ball. However, if we posit a different situation—for example, a brand new ball that belongs to an older sibling who has explicitly said, "Don't touch my stuff!"—then the authority would not be there.

Time, place, and conditions are all concepts that were previously explored in the modeling of sequence and order. Thus the ideas are not new; they simply need to be re-explored in the context of the idea of *opportunity*. In the case of the simplest form model of *self* picking up the ball, the time is now, the place is here, and condition to act exists because the ball is on the ground in front of *self*.

In discussions and environmental exploration with the facilitator, the client will explore examples of both the absence and existence of each of the elements. For example, a person may be hungry at five o'clock, but will not eat until six o'clock, because six is the time set for dinner. The place for eating dinner is the dining room table, not the bathroom or the floor in the den. The conditions for eating dinner are that the table must be set, the family must be gathered, and the meal must be prepared. The *motivation* to eat has been in place for an hour, but it is only at six o'clock, when every family member has come to the table, and the meal has been prepared and laid out in serving dishes, that the *opportunity* to enjoy the meal exists.

In the clay model, *opportunity* is the ball on the table in front of the primary (largest) model of *self*. That is the same ball that was used to represent *need*—but with the addition of the elements of *intention, skill,* and *knowledge,* it now represents *opportunity*.

The entire construction, taken together, is *ability.*

The understanding of *ability* lays a strong foundation for the future. With the facilitator, the client will likely be exploring the ideas of simple abilities—the things that he can do, and the abilities he observes in others. For example, he may have the ability to play the piano; his father has the ability to drive a car. But the Davis program itself has instilled new skills and knowledge, which will in turn create new opportunities.

The autistic client is emerging from a state of disability to one where he will have or acquire the same degree of ability and self-sufficiency that non-autistics take for granted. With the Davis model, he also has a framework to know what he needs at each step of the way.

Control—ability to cause change

The last common concept to be mastered is *control*, defined as "ability to cause change." *Control* is linked to the concepts of *motivation* and *ability* by the shared root concept of *change*. If the client understands each of the ideas represented in the model, then all pieces are already in place.

Within the existing model, *change* is demonstrated simply by moving the large *self* model so that it depicts *self* in the act of causing change. With the clay ball model, that would mean simply that the clay *self* bends over to pick up the ball that was initially used to represent *need*, and then *opportunity*. The three concepts together show the process of turning an idea or desire into action.

They also once again echo the triad of *mind*, *body*, and *lifeforce*. Motivation and its energy root provide the force; ability with its continue root provides the learning and experience; and the concept of control brings the idea and knowledge into the realm of the physical world.

An Advanced Concept—Responsibility

The final Identity Development concept to be modeled is *responsibility*, defined as "ability and motivation to control." The client has already modeled each of the concepts that are contained within the definition: ability, motivation, control. The last model incorporates those three ideas and links them together.

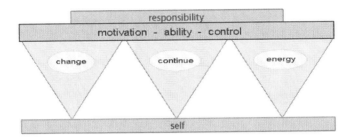

Given that the common concepts have already been modeled, there is no need to add to the existing clay model of *control.* Instead, the facilitator will have the client remove the word "control" and the dominant arrow, and then identify each of the concepts at all levels that can be found within the model. The facilitator will bring her client to an understanding that the convergence of *motivation, ability,* and *control* within *self* is *responsibility,* and that the model as a whole represents that concept.

The facilitator will then explore the final concept of responsibility with her client, identifying things and situations that he has responsibility for, as well as the areas where he does not have responsibility. Through that dialogue, the client will realize that whenever he does not have responsibility, it is because he lacks some facet of either ability or motivation.

Before coming to the Davis program, the autistic client will have significant areas in his life where he has not exercised responsibility, either because of the direct or the indirect impact of his autism. The autism will have directly stood in the way in situations where it prevented him from perceiving or understanding his environment in a way that would allow him to exert control. Additionally, as an indirect result of the autism, the client will have been deprived of the opportunity to gain necessary skills in many areas. His life has been constrained in many ways.

With the modeling—and mastery—of *responsibility* -- the Davis program gives each client the key to his own future success in life. That is what is meant by "the ability to fully participate in life." Not only is the person brought into the realm of understanding his world, but he now also has a process that can be used to guide his life and forge an independent path.

Davis Facilitator Elizabeth Shier shares this story about one young boy she worked with:

"I am keeping in close touch with my first client, seven-year-old Ryan, who finished the concepts through responsibility. Last week his Mom walked into my office with tears in her eyes, hugged me so hard I could not breathe and said, 'Ryan shared with his younger brother and nobody told him he had to! You have given me my son.' She was overwhelmed at the changes she's seen in Ryan's relationships with his siblings.

"Ryan has also made a friend at school and the boys got into some trouble—leaving the classroom behind the teacher's back and hiding in the bathroom giggling like mad. When they got caught, he didn't try to blame the other child. At first, his parents were mortified, but they now realize that kind of shared planning with another child wasn't possible for him in the past. And he's never taken the blame for anything before so they were happy to see that he understood his role in the trouble and he readily accepted his consequence. He has since found better ways to make plans with his new friend."

As the story illustrates, the client who has gained an understanding of the Davis concepts does not always behave in ways that adults would prefer. A young person who is capable of exercising control in his life is also capable of breaking rules and testing limits. But Ryan also was able to accept blame and to understand the consequences of his acts—something that simply would have been beyond his ability to comprehend before working through the concepts.

In sum, Ryan started behaving like a "normal" child, rather than a child with a disability. *Responsibility,* and all of the concepts encompassed within it, had become a part of his identity.

Identity Development Integration

With the completion of the final Identity Development concept, all of the parts are in place. The client now has a basic mastery of each of the concepts needed for development of a new facet of his identity: a person capable of understanding himself and exercising control over his environment, ready to accept and exercise responsibility in his life. He has the understanding, the knowledge, and the wisdom needed to take this step.

All that remains is to set the parts in motion. The client will need to use and apply the concepts to completing a task in a real world setting. Once that is done, the concepts will have been fully integrated into his core identity.

Because the concept modeling culminated with the idea of *responsibility,* integration of the concepts will require a setting in which the client can assume and exercise responsibility. That is usually done with the "Establishing Order" exercise. For a child or adolescent, the ideal setting is to be given responsibility for establishing order within his own bedroom.

Because the Davis goals are to provide tools for life, the child's zone of responsibility should continue long after the Davis program has concluded. As the modeling has demonstrated, in order to exercise responsibility, a person must also have control. That means that if the child takes responsibility for establishing order in his own bedroom, the parents must be willing to allow the child to assume that responsibility on a long term, permanent basis. If a parent is unwilling to cede that much control to a child, or the child's living quarters are not appropriate for that—for example, if the child shares a bedroom with an older sibling—then a different zone of control can be assigned. For example, the child may be given responsibility for establishing order within his own desk or chest of drawers.

Before a person can exercise responsibility, he must have the knowledge and skill needed for the task. To ensure that the child is ready to establish order in his own space, the facilitator will work with him to develop a list of steps that are needed to establish order in any environment. The facilitator will first have her client assemble a jigsaw puzzle on his own, giving instruction as to steps to be followed, such as first turning all the pieces face up, then isolating pieces with an edge, and so on until the puzzle has been completed. This exercise helps reinforce the idea that to create order out of disorder, a sequential, step-by-step process should be followed.

The facilitator will then work with her client to establish order among a selected group of objects gathered for the purpose of the exercise, such as the contents of a desk drawer. The objects will simply be heaped in the center of a desk or table. The client is given the task of determining the proper place and position for each object in turn. The facilitator guides and helps develop a list of questions to ask about each object. From this exercise, the client has been given a simple framework that can be applied to the task of establishing order in any environment. The sequence for establishing order has nine steps:

1) isolate an individual thing;

2) identify what it is;

3) determine its condition;

4) based on its identity and condition, determine the best place for it to be in;

5) assign it that place;

6) determine what position it should occupy in that place;

7) assign it that position;

8) put it in that position in that place;

9) repeat this sequence until order is established in the environment.

For this process, the facilitator or other helper will be with the client in his room—or the area of his agreed zone of responsibility—to guide him through the steps of establishing order in a real-life situation. The client will generally have a written copy of the nine steps, and under the guidance and encouragement of the facilitator will apply those to the task of organizing his space. The facilitator will encourage him to shift to relying on his memory of the steps, rather than the written list, and over time the thought process will become automatic.

Although Davis has broken down the process into nine separate elements, the actual process is similar to what most people would naturally do when tidying up an area; individuals with autism or ADHD simply need extra help at the outset to gain that skill.[66]

Though the facilitator is present, the client exercises control by personally making the decision as to what place

---

[66] A detailed description of the Establishing Order exercise is contained in Chapter 16 of *The Gift of Learning*. (Davis and Braun, Gift of Learning 2003)

and position is appropriate for each object. If he decides that his socks belong in the bottom drawer, then the bottom drawer will be used, even if his mother has always placed socks in the top drawer. The essence of *responsibility* is *control;* and the person who establishes order must be the one to make the decisions.

When working with older teenagers and adults, a facilitator will sometimes use an alternate approach to the task of identity integration. Often, the older client will already have some area of their life which is their assigned "responsibility," but where they have experienced difficulty. For example, a teenager may have household chores that are expected but not completed; an adult may be experiencing difficulty following through with regular workplace duties. The facilitator can help address those issues, providing the dual benefit of a path to identity integration together with helping the client to confront and overcome an existing life barrier. The process of resolving those problems also reinforces the learning that has already taken place, because the facilitator will need to help her client determine what element of the Davis construct is missing. Is the problem one of lack of motivation? Or lack of ability, due to lack of requisite knowledge or skill? In the course of those explorations, the client will not only address the problem at hand, but will also be able to see how the Davis concepts are successfully applied to real life situations.

The end result is that the Davis program has done away with the "disability" aspect of autism. The idea of "disability" carries with it a belief that the person is incapable of doing something—for example, a person who has lost the use of his legs has a disability because he cannot walk. But in some cases, the internalized belief of incapacity becomes a barrier in and of itself. The individual comes to assume that his disability represents an insurmountable barrier, and so he accepts his limitations rather than take the steps needed for change. Davis provides a roadmap that allows the individual to form and carry out a plan of action to overcome his disabilities. When these concepts are put into action, they are self-reinforcing. Each success builds confidence and the ability to take on other challenges.

With the completion of Identity Development, the client emerges as a person who is capable of understanding, addressing, and coping with a normal array of life events and experiences. He has traveled from a world of chaos and confusion and become a confident and capable human being.

The Davis program is not finished, because the work that has been completed is one of self-actualization. The essential barrier of autism is difficulty with social communication and relationships, something yet to be addressed. However, self-understanding is an important prerequisite to social understanding and engagement.[67] Often it is best for a period of days, weeks, or even months to elapse between completion of the Identity Development phase and the final stage of Social Integration. Usually the client will know when he is ready, and then arrange to meet with the facilitator for the final stage of the program.

---

[67] (Lombardo and Baron-Cohen, The role of the self in mindblindness in autism 2011)

Chapter 11

Social Integration

The third and final phase of the Davis Autism Approach provides a foundation for autistic individuals to form and maintain social relationships. This is again done by using clay to model a set of general concepts. Under the guidance of the facilitator, the client will first focus on the concept of *another* and *others*, move on to the idea of a *relationship,* then explore four basic types of relationships, and finally address the idea of *right* and *wrong.*

The Davis program is not designed to teach a client social skills, morals, or cultural norms, but rather to provide the client with an *understanding* of a set of basic concepts that influence and guide interactions with others. Through the concept modeling and environmental explorations during the Identity Development sequence, the client has already been encouraged to observe and think about the motivations and actions of other people. From the point of modeling of *consequence*, much of the Davis program will already have enabled the client to gain greater insight into his own behavior and its impact on others around him. Additionally, he has been encouraged to observe the behavior of others, and to notice and draw inferences from their gestures and facial expressions. However, the focus remained ego-centric, with the central and paramount goal being self-understanding and self-actualization.

In the context of social relationships, the focus must shift to awareness, recognition, and respect of the wants, needs, and motivations of others. The autist must learn to see himself as part of something larger than himself: a pair, a trio, a group. He will need to be able to recognize the relationship itself as being something that is living and dynamic, something that can be preserved and nurtured through the interactions of the individuals involved. Through that understanding, he will be able to transition from a self-centered existence to becoming a participating member of his community.

Another and Others

The process begins with the placing of a model of *self* on the table. The client then adds a model of a second person, to be designated *another*. To cement the understanding that this model represents another human being, the client will point to the clay figure and say, "You represent *another*, meaning an individual separate from *me*. You represent every *experience* the individual has ever had, all the *knowledge*, all the *wisdom* and all the *understanding*."

The next step is the modeling of several figures, to create a group representing *others*. The same process will be followed: "You represent *others* meaning individuals separate from *me*. You represent every *experience* each individual separate from me has ever had, all the *knowledge*, all the *wisdom*, and all the *understanding*." In this way, the client is guided to recognize and consider other persons as separate, individually motivated individuals.

The repetition of this phrasing, worded to parallel the earlier identification of *self*, naturally draws the client's attention to the idea that other people exist as individuals separate from himself, each with their own set of experiences drawn from their own knowledge, wisdom and understanding. Because the script parallels the words used to identify the *self* model, it also reinforces the idea that other individuals are very much like self, even though they are also separate beings.

However, it is not the goal of the Davis program to affirmatively teach "theory of mind." The client will draw whatever inferences from the social integration concepts as are natural for him at the time. The program goal is to provide the foundation that will enable him to form and participate in meaningful relationships with others. He will not be able to do that without also understanding the separate and independent nature of others, but it is probably not necessary that he explicitly contemplate their thought processes until he is actually meeting and engaging with real people rather than clay figures.

The facilitator will continue to discuss each concept with her client, but the environmental explorations are no longer needed or appropriate. Because the focus has shifted to a concern with *others*, it is no longer possible for the client to gain full mastery of the ideas to be explored while working with the facilitator. The *others* are not there to participate, so the experiential learning that goes along with forming relationships and interacting with others cannot be achieved in a one-on-one context with the facilitator. The facilitator can only provide one prong of the triad of mastery: *understanding*, or information gained from observation. At this stage, the facilitator is leading and teaching. Later, the client will be able to explore on his own, in real life settings with real people.

The Role of Self in Relationships

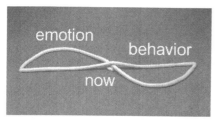

The client will next set the model of *others* aside briefly, to focus again on *self*, this time in preparation for understanding his own role in forming relationships. The facilitator begins by having the client create a symbolic representation of the emotions and behavior of *self* as he moves through time. This is done by starting with a small dot of clay placed on the table to represent the idea of the *now*, the present moment in time. Overlaid on this will be a straight piece of clay which is joined at the ends and intersected in the center by an overlapping clay rope shaped like a sine wave.

The wavy strand of clay represents the client's *emotion*. He has already mastered the concept of *emotion*, defined as his self-created energy, and does not need to master it again. Rather, the clay is now used as a symbol of an idea he already understands.

The straight line represents the client's *behavior*—defined as "the way I act or conduct myself"—or, when the word is identified separately from the clay, the way *one* acts or conducts *oneself*. In this way the Davis definition again subtly draws the client's attention to the idea that *behavior* is a concept that applies both to himself and to the actions of others.

Next a transitional arrow is added to the model, positioned at the *now* dot and pointing away from *self*. The client identifies the arrow with the words, "you show my movement through time."

The client then retrieves his model of *another* and places it at the point of the *arrow,* in front of and facing *self*. This becomes the model of *relationship*—the inter-action of one (or "me") with another. The client now has a model that shows *self* in the same context that others might see him, as a person who carries with him a set of emotions and behaviors. He can also see from the model that his ability to build and participate in relationships is tied closely to his emotions and behaviors.

He is ready to explore the idea of different types of relationships.

Four Forms of Relationships

Davis has identified four fundamental types of rela-tionships. Each is based on the underlying element of commonality that connects the individual with another person or group with whom he interacts. Every relation-ship that a person has can be defined by one or more of these forms. The form of the relationship guides the behaviors of the individuals within the relationship.

A common characteristic of autism is the tendency to interpret statements literally and to take the actions of others at face value. Socially adept neurotypical individ-uals tend to conform their words and actions to the expectations of others, often shading the truth to suit the situation, perhaps relying on euphemism to avoid offending others, or using humor or sarcasm to get their point across. The autist, lacking guile, is constantly at risk of misinterpreting the intent and motives of others.

The Davis framework will allow the client to contextualize the behavior of others depending on the pattern of interaction that defines each relationship. An understanding of each type of relationship will help the client know what sort of behavior is expected of him, and what to anticipate or expect from others within that relationship.

The first model is a relationship based on *trust*, defined as "the feeling that another is equal to self." Because this relationship is based on an emotion within self and another, it is represented in the model with a feeling bubble attached to both models. Each feeling bubble contains two small figures, with an equal sign between them. This represents the idea that each individual in the relationship shares the feeling that the other person is their equal.

Trust can be the foundation of a relationship between one person and another. A person can have many friends, but the *trust* relationship will be established separately as to each. The *trust* relationship is the hallmark of a true friendship.

Understanding the importance of the mutuality of the trust relationship will help the client evaluate future relationships. Autists sometimes get in trouble because they are overly trusting; they may not realize that a person who seems friendly may end up mistreating them. Although the client will never be able to read the mind of another person, the Davis model helps him to ask himself the right questions as he embarks on new relationships.

The second form of re-
lationship is one based on
belief. Belief also stems from
a shared emotion or internalized feeling, but belief
can be the foundation of a
relationship with one person
or with many. Davis defines

belief as "what is felt to be actual or real." An obvious
example would be a relationship among members of a
shared religion, but the Davis definition is broad enough
to encompass any type of shared opinion. For example, it
could be the shared feeling that bowling is a fun and
enjoyable activity, which might prompt the individual to
join with others in a bowling league. Because the belief
can be anything, it can be represented by clay balls; these
are modeled within two separated feeling bubbles, linked
separately to *self* and *another.*

In looking at the models, we can see that the belief-
based relationship requires a shared feeling about
something, without having the mutual regard that exists in
the trust-based relationship. Two individuals can share
the belief that bowling is fun, and perhaps bowl on the
same team, even if they do not like each other or socialize
outside of the bowling alley.

The remaining two forms of relationship are based on
concepts that originate outside of *self,* created for the
benefit of groups of individuals and for society.

The first is *agree,* defined as "what is thought to be
actual or real." The concept of *agree* allows for a relationship with many others, and will guide the individual to
behave in a way that is in keeping with the shared
expectations of others. That is, *agree* is more than merely
the idea of a contractual arrangement; it includes the
mutual understanding of expectations in a variety of

settings. One common example would be making and keeping an appointment. The interaction between a store clerk and customer is another example: they each agree that the customer will be entitled to remove objects from the store upon payment of an agreed amount of money. The *agree* model is similar to the *belief* model, but each figure has a thought bubble rather than a feeling bubble, because the agreement is based on shared understanding of facts rather than emotion.

The final model is a relationship based on *rules*. Rules are "regulations that establish boundaries of acceptable behavior." The concept of rules allows for relationships and behaviors with *all* others. Rules are generally established to promote the functioning of the group. For example, a law may be enacted by a government body to limit the acts of individuals in order to protect the rights of others. The same rationale would apply to the set of rules set by a teacher in a classroom; for example, a rule that students must raise their hand and wait to be called upon before speaking. This concept can be modeled in clay by using markers to delineate boundaries along the *behavior* line, adding a small model of a book or tablet to represent the idea of a regulation.

High functioning autistic individuals are often frustrated by difficulty understanding and adhering to a broad range of unspoken standards and expectations that govern social interaction. They may try to compensate by trying to memorize a growing list of social rules taught to them by parents and tutors, or gained from experience along the way, but they are stymied by a seemingly endless list of new rules to be learned.

The Davis model instead provides a simple way for the individual to contextualize his social relationships, and the behavioral expectations that go along with each. A relationship is strengthened and will en-dure when each person behaves in a way that is consistent with and supports the element of commonality that underlies that relationship. The Davis model may lead the client to realize that within a trust-based relationship, his behavior should be grounded on treating the other individual (his equal) as he himself would want to be treated; and to recognize and consider the needs of the group with a rule-based relationship. The facilitator will help him during the modeling to think about examples of the different forms, as well as to understand that the forms overlap and can exist together within any particular relationship. Later, on his own, he will be able to use his ability to categorize relationships to help guide his behavior. He will certainly make mistakes along the way, but he has a tool that makes it easier to apply the lessons he learns to their appropriate contexts.

The conceptual approach learned with Davis will also help the individual correctly gauge the importance of his actions, and those of others, within the context of various relationships. Many high-functioning autists agonize unnecessarily over a minor social *faux pas*; not only does the autist have difficulty knowing how to behave in a given situation, but he lacks the ability to know and appreciate the likely consequences of errors he makes. With the Davis model, he can focus on the issues that really matter: he understands which behaviors will likely be shrugged off and ignored by others, and which will threaten the continuation of the relationship. Similarly, he will know when he needs to take action to rectify an error.

The Final Piece: Bad and Good, Wrong and Right

After completion of the models depicting the four categories of relationships, there is one final segment: modeling of the ideas *bad* and *good*, and *wrong* and *right*.

Early in Ron Davis' career, long before he began to develop his program for autism, he worked with a young autistic girl I will call Malika. The girl was the granddaughter of Ron's colleague, Dr. Fatima Ali, and thus Ron came to know her very well over the years. Malika particularly loved to watch the Disney animated film, *Pinocchio,* and Ron assumed that she was entranced by the idea of the little wooden puppet who wanted to become human. One day he asked what part of the story she liked best, and she surprised him by saying that she liked Jiminy Cricket, the character who is appointed by the Blue Fairy to act as Pinocchio's conscience, to guide him to know the difference between right and wrong. Malika explained, "I don't have a conscience, and that is what I need."

The final step of the Davis relationship concepts supplies the client with the ability to create his own conscience, to guide his future actions in the context of his relationships with the intent to do what is *right*. Understanding the idea of *right* as opposed to *wrong* by itself doesn't guarantee that the person will always make the correct choices, but it does mean that the individual will be using his own acquired knowledge, wisdom, and understanding to make choices for appropriate reasons. The person will not be simply acting based on memorized sets of social rules or a desire to fit in or be accepted by others.

This is not an effort to teach or impose a set of morals, as the Davis modeling does not provide a set of rules or examples. The facilitator may discuss examples in the context of helping the client understand the concepts, but would do so in a way that would guide the client toward further exploration and understanding. The Davis goal is to imbue each client with the *ability*—as well as the *responsibility*—to exercise his own judgment to determine what is *right* within the context of his relationships with others.

Davis defines each concept very simply, as follows:

Bad: not in support of survival

Good: in support of survival

Wrong: an action not in support of survival

Right: an action in support of survival

"Survival" is used in the definition because it is the base concept from the second construction: "survival" represents the way we, as humans, experience *continue*. To *survive* means to *continue as self*.

In the clay relationship model, survival is represented by adding models symbolizing life and death to the relationship paradigm, along with clay arrows representing emotions and behaviors that support (or do not support) survival.

With this model, the idea of *bad* or *good* is tied directly to emotions and actions of *self*, which are represented by the straight and curved lines of clay on which the model of *self* is standing. These concepts are also depicted within the context of a relationship with *another*.

The next step is to model *wrong*, then *right*. In each case the negative concept (bad, wrong) is modeled prior to the positive concept (good, right), because that order of modeling will lead the facilitator and client to end with the positive model. That is, the very last model that will be constructed is one that depicts the idea of *right* behavior.

Wrong is simply an *action* that is *bad*, that is, *not in support of survival*. And the final concept modeled, *right*, is an *action* that is *good*—*in support of survival*. Because this model is created in the context of a relationship with *another*, the idea of promoting mutual survival is also implicit in the model. A relationship works when all participants are able to *continue as self*. The client is making the *right* choice when his actions foster both his own ability to continue as self, and the ability of others to continue in the same way.

The client who has modeled all of the relationship concepts still must gain the knowledge and wisdom that will come only with actively participating within relationships. He will make mistakes, because mistakes are part of the learning process—he may stand too closely to others in a social group, speak too loudly, forget to make eye contact, or arrive to a social gathering dressed inappropriately. But he will be making those mistakes with a new understanding and set of underlying skills. Just as the nine steps for establishing order gave him the ability to ask himself the questions needed to create order in his environment, without setting forth specific rules for the handling of dirty socks, the relationship concepts provide an internalized, analytic framework that will guide the learning process.

The breadth and simplicity of the Davis-based understanding will make it easier to know when to apply the lessons learned in one context to another, and to develop the ability to understand and anticipate how the actions taken as an individual will impact others, and how others are likely to respond.

If the client has embraced the concept of striving to do what is *good* and *right*, then his own behavior will likely fit within the "golden rule:" he will treat others as he himself wants to be treated. His actions will be ethical, because he will strive to avoid doing harm. And he will also be able to protect himself within relationships—to recognize when a relationship is going sour, or when others are taking advantage of him or treating him unfairly—because he will be able to focus on the broader context of the relationship and the impact of others' behavior as well as his own.

The client who has completed the final step of the Davis program is not finished with the learning process. On the contrary, he is just beginning—but he is now equipped with the tools and concepts needed to function effectively and independently—in short, to begin to participate fully in the life he will make for himself.

Chapter 12

The Way Forward

The Davis Autism Approach provides a new paradigm for addressing the internal barriers with social functioning that are the hallmark characteristic of autism. The program stems from the experience and ideas of a successful adult with a childhood history of autism, and as such is designed with an inherent respect and understanding for the autistic perspective. The approach has been developed and refined through collective practical experience accumulated over many years.

The stated goal of the program—to enable autistic individuals to "participate fully in life"—is best illustrated through the actual experience of autistic individuals, their family members, and the facilitators who guided them.

The Davis Difference

"In this program I worked with clay to learn concepts like 'me,' 'time,' 'order,' 'sequence,' and most importantly to me, 'relationship.' My facilitator also taught me how to release and relax, and mentally anchor myself to this world so that I can

stop myself from becoming disoriented, or from accidentally day dreaming. I've also learned how to recognize and control my anxiety attacks and temper tantrums. When I feel them coming on, I can choose to change my thoughts and release, and it would be like nothing was bothering me to begin with! I now know how to set safe boundaries with people so that I don't become overwhelmed by their emotions, or get taken advantage of. I can verbally express my feelings in ways I never could before. Dealing with large crowds of people is still exhausting, but it's not terrifying and overwhelming the way it used to be."[68]

The Davis Autism Approach stands on its own as a unique method for enabling and empowering autistic individuals. The program can lead to profound changes in functional ability, manifested through changed attitudes and behavior, well beyond the expectations of other programs. At the same time, the program avoids direct efforts to change, manipulate, or coerce behavior, and is not premised on an effort to teach the autistic client to think or act as if he were not autistic. Many high functioning autists are rightfully wary and resistant to the efforts of others to change the way they think and feel. The changes that come with a Davis program come naturally, as a result of the learning process and development of new skills and insights. Davis provides an avenue for increased self-awareness and social engagement, while at the same time preserving the integrity of the individual.

---

[68] Posted to a *Facebook* group, August 1, 2009; Retrieved from https://www.facebook.com/groups/6567263146/ February 26, 2012

Some key elements that distinguish the Davis program from others are:

1. An Autistic Source

Because of Ron Davis' own history of childhood autism, his ideas are products of his autistic experience and thought processes. Davis understands that his experience is unique; no two autists are alike, and it is impossible to generalize from one to another. But Davis' background did give him a sensitivity and awareness as to how the experience of autism impacts behavior.

For example, Davis understands that many prevalent beliefs about autism are misguided. For instance, it is commonly asserted that autism is associated with a lack of empathy. But the autistic experience often includes extreme sensitivity and reactivity to the emotions and feelings of others. Avoidance behaviors such as retreating from others, or avoiding touch or eye contact, are not a sign of indifference, but instead are an indication that the autist is feeling overwhelmed.[69]

Davis also understands from his own experience that an effective learning process does not require an autist to mimic the behavior of neurotypical individuals or to change the way he thinks. Autists can learn and progress

---

[69] One theorist draws a distinction between "cognitive" and "emotional" empathy. "Cognitive empathy" is the ability to understand and predict the behavior of another, and equates with "theory of mind." "Emotional empathy" is an emotional response of one person that stems from and parallels the emotional state of another. From the autobiographical accounts of many autistic adults, as well as observations of behavior of autistic children, there is strong evidence that autists commonly experience a surfeit of emotional empathy which leads to feelings of fear, discomfort, and confusion. (Smith 2009) See also, the "intense world" theory of autism (Markram and Markram 2010)

with an approach suited to their cognitive strengths. Their behavior will change if and when the reason for that behavior disappears.

2. Developed from Practice

Although a formalized structure for the Davis Autism Approach was set for the first time in 2008, the specific methodology and tools have been in use since the early 1980's. The structured program as it now stands represents the collective thinking of a dozen individuals with extensive experience working with Davis techniques, with children and adults of all ages, in multiple languages and countries, as well as the continuing input of dozens more who have received training in the method and are actively working with autistic clients.

It was natural for Davis to consider developing a program around modeling words and concepts in clay, as that approach had worked personally for him—but the clay techniques were retained and refined because they worked, not because Davis thought of them. Some program elements described in this book were developed precisely to solve problems that cropped up along the way. For example, the Alignment procedure was developed when it became apparent that some individuals were unable to follow the visualization script used for the Davis Orientation procedure. The practice of including a clay model of "self" in all Concept Mastery models began with a young boy who could not learn from modeling the idea of "consequence" without including himself.

3. Supported by Tools for Orientation, Balance, and Stress-Release

The Davis program begins with specific training to enable an individual to harmonize perceptions, control and sustain attention focus, release stress, and regulate energy level, as well as a simple skill-building exercise with Koosh balls geared to improving balance and coordination. The Davis orientation training techniques are unique, but their mechanism is similar to neurofeedback: through mental training, an individual gains improved ability to regulate mental state and attention focus.[70] However, because most of the Davis orientation tools rely on short, simple, direct instructions, with the individual learning to use their own bodily sensations for feedback, the Davis techniques can generally be taught and learned very quickly. The recorded tone sequence for auditory orientation can be played on standard portable playback devices. No specialized equipment is needed.[71] Each of the Davis tools can be practiced and reinforced regularly at home as well as during sessions with a facilitator.

4. Guided, Participatory, and Integrated Mastery of Essential Concepts

The heart of the Davis Autism Approach is the guided mastery of key concepts, which provide the missing elements necessary to develop a distinct sense of "self," and a natural, core identity. These concepts provide an understanding of both the external world, and the internal world of thoughts and feelings. The program ends with a set of concepts focused on the individual's role within relationships with others. Each concept rests on a simple idea, and concepts are presented sequentially, with each

---

[70] Neurofeedback training has been shown to improve executive functioning and social behavior among autistic children. (Kouijzer, van Schie, et al. 2010) (Kouijzer, de Moor, et al. 2009)

[71] In contrast, neurofeedback typically requires many hours of practice through trial-and-error with a computer interface. For example, students in one research study received 40 half-hour, twice-weekly sessions. Because the training was machine-dependent, there would have been no opportunity for practice and reinforcement between sessions. (Kouijzer, de Moor, et al. 2009)

building upon previously mastered ideas. The concepts are drawn from experience rather than psychological theory. Instead of theorizing about what typical developmental landmarks should be replicated for autistic clients, the Davis concepts were developed from practical experience working with children and adults.

With this approach, the process of learning is natural and can be easily paced and geared to the needs of the individual. The use of clay ensures active participation by the learner. Clay modeling also provides a method of depicting abstract concepts that overcomes limitations in language facility, and is geared to visual learning strengths that are common with autism.[72]

The guided exploration and dialogue expands and reinforces the insights gained from clay modeling, and helps the autist relate the concepts to observations of people and events. The autist is also gently guided to focus greater attention on other people encountered during explorations, using observation both as a way of exemplifying and extending the ideas explored during clay modeling.

Because of the fixed set of concepts and order of presentation, progress through the program can be easily ascertained by the facilitator, the autist, and family members. Progress is measured by the autist's ability to identify and explain each concept in turn, both in clay and in the real world. Because a similar set of steps is followed for mastery of each concept, along with repeated use of language and clay symbols, the autist is likely to become more comfortable with the approach and work more

---

[72] Autistic individuals seem to have an enhanced ability to form, access, and manipulate visual mental representations. (Soulières, Zeffiro, et al. 2011) Visual processes seem to play a prominent role in autistic reasoning and ability to assimilate information. (Soulières, Dawson and Samson, et al. 2009)

efficiently as the program progresses.

5. Focus on Self-Understanding

Ron Davis knew from his own childhood that his autism equated to a sense of "being everything and nothing" at the same time, and that he had to first take the steps of individuation, and then identity development, before he could function in the world and relate to others. So it seemed obvious to him that gaining an understanding of "self" would naturally be the first step any autist would need to take before being able to adapt to and function within the social world with others.

Academic researchers have only very recently begun to hone in on the importance of self-conceptualization, and the role it plays in the thought processes and functional behavior of autistic individuals.[73] Researchers now assert that the "self" is "one of the most important topics in autism research," but the research-derived ideas have not yet been used to develop new therapeutic approaches to autism.[74] Most therapeutic interventions for autism have been focused more directly on the autist's ability to engage with others, and generally rest on teaching new behaviors, such as encouraging eye contact or practicing conversation skills.

The Davis program is built on the explicit exploration of concepts related to *self* and self-understanding. In addition to the potential benefit the approach offers to

---

[73] The first research study to explore self-awareness in autism appears to be a report published in 1999, involving three adults with Asperger's who were asked to note and describe their own thoughts. (Frith and Happé 1999)

[74] (Lombardo and Baron-Cohen, The role of the self in mindblindness in autism 2011) See also, (Hobson, Explaining autism: Ten reasons to focus on the developing self 2010)

autistic individuals, the Davis program is also likely to inform and influence future research into the role that self-cognition plays in the development of social understanding, which is elusive for autistic individuals.

Case Study: Diary of a Davis Program

Davis Facilitator Karen LoGiudice kept a diary of her progress working with a young woman in her early twenties. Amber lived in a group home and was enrolled in a day program providing activities such as art projects. When Karen first met her, she was very quiet, and answered most questions with a quick "Yes" or "No." When she arrived to start her program, Amber's parents were concerned about behavior issues that were causing difficulty at the group home. Amber showed little interest in the activities and conversations of others around her, and her physical coordination skills were very poor. Her parents regularly drove her to and from the sessions with Karen. The Davis program was completed over the course of fifteen days, scheduled in three separate week-long blocks, spread out over the course of six months. The extended scheduling gave Karen the opportunity to observe the changes which occurred in Amber's life between sessions, as the seeds planted during each program week took root and flourished.

Week 1, October. Completed Individuation. Identity Development concepts through "Survive":

> **Day 1:** Amber is super quiet and not very verbal. However, I think she may have more language than she appears to have. Amber took well to **Release** and **Alignment, Auditory Fine Tuning** and **Koosh**. When she listened to the auditory orientation ding sound, a sense of calm came over her. Mum was shocked to hear that she was able

to catch the Koosh ball while balanced on one foot. Her fine-motor skills are rough—so the clay is not entirely easy for her. The quality of her clay work improved a bit throughout the day, especially with the letters. I think she is opening up to it as she gets more experience.

Day 2: *Amber came in happy. Dad reported that she was excited about the Koosh balls and he is also surprised by her ability to catch the balls. He said that she and Mum worked on finding **change** on the way home. She also is responding well to listening to the ding. She listened three times today (the whole eight minute track). Amber showed signs of individuation this afternoon. At a break, for the first time, she addressed me directly with a question about noise at her day program. She said that the other people make too much noise, and it bothered her very much. She then went on to say that another woman calls her terrible names and that she doesn't like it. She said that it is not all right for the woman to treat her that way.*

Day 3: *Amber came in happy. As we reviewed **consequence, cause-effect, before-after**, I was confident that she had it! This was further confirmed as we worked through **time**. We took our first "out of the office exploration" to the hardware store and Dunkin Donuts. We measured all kinds of things (observing, at cause, and at effect) with the stop watch. I noticed that the clay is getting a lot easier. Amber is more confident with making the models, although she still needs guidance. Mum reported that, for the first time ever, Amber went up to her and said, "Do you want to know what we worked on today?" and* *then went over the concepts step by step. Mum said she wondered, "Is this the same Amber I've known for twenty-two years?"*

Day 4: *Simplest form of **time** was not easy. Amber seemed really tired after doing it. We took a long break. **Sequence** seemed to go well, with many examples to work with. Dad was very enthusiastic about the program and said he saw a glint in Amber's eyes when they came back from lunch he had never seen before.*

Day 5: *Review of **sequence** was awesome. Not only did Amber solidly have the meaning, but she was intently looking at the clay to show each piece of it. It was the first time I saw intent in her. **Order** and **disorder** also went well. We went to the grocery store to explore the concept in the environment and it was great. We also talked about **order** and **disorder** in relation to her tools and certain situations. It was great to hear her relating to how she could use them in her life—"What would be the proper condition for you in ___ situation? What tools would you use with that? What would you have to do to give yourself **order**?" She answered these questions with ease. **Continue** and **survive** rounded out our week—went well. Mum was surprised and very impressed to see us playing Koosh, seeing Amber balanced like a rock and reacting to the balls coming at her.*

Week 2, February. Identity Development concepts through "Emotion:"

Day 6: *To my delight, the change in Amber is amazing! Her eyes are clear and have a sparkle that was not there before. She is making eye* *contact, wanted to tell me all about what she had been doing since she left. (She secured a JOB ... which she had never been allowed to do—but with the progress she has made, now can!) In our review of the concepts we'd done thus far, she had completely retained all of them—we had so much fun looking at the pictures of her models from the first week, and she was able to identify all the different parts. Dad relayed that the behavior issues had almost entirely cleared up at the group home. It was clear, from the outcome of the situation, that Amber had integrated **consequence** since we last worked together.*

__Day 7: Perception__ and __thought__ went well. Amber's fine motor skills are getting better. Clay seems to be getting a little easier. She is starting to open up more and making much more eye contact.

*__Day 8:__ Finished **experience** and had a really fun "field trip" to discover some new experiences together. It was a bonding exercise. Amber seems to be more interested in other people. She made some comment about the little store we found—like that it was a place her grandmother would like to go to. She made eye contact with the man behind the register, and seemed to be watching me as I interacted and talked with him.*

*__Day 9:__ All of the concepts seemed to go well. I was impressed at how easily she picked up **energy** and **force**.*

*__Day 10:__ We got through a lot of concepts today. I wasn't expecting **emotion** to go so quickly. The exploration was fun. Amber's facial expressions changed as we saw different emotions on different people. This was where her first unsolicited con-*

versation came. At McDonald's, she saw a middle-aged man walk up to a little old woman and say, "Well hello, there, young lady!" The old woman was delighted. Amber's eye darted and looked straight at mine as if to say, "I understood that that was a joke!" She giggled. What followed was even more stunning. Amber began telling me about her grandmother. She went into a long, detailed story of how her grandmother was from Scotland and met her husband during the war when he was serving in the army. Later that day, I recalled the story to Amber's mother—who was taken aback, and said, "Amber told you all that?!" I later found out that the family literally had no idea that Amber knew that story and were shocked that she had actually taken in any of that information.

Week 3, April. Completion, Identity Development through Establishing Order; Social Integration with Relationship Concepts:

*Day 11: It was great to hear that Amber has started her job! She is SO happy. She is now able to work without immediate staff supervision. **Skill** went really well. We went to the arcade. Amber was having a blast. Her eyes sparkled, she felt accomplished, and she was learning and improving with the games each time she played.*

Day 12: Good day today. Amber was discussing our planned trip to the group home tomorrow with Mum and me. She was very adamant about certain facts—who was going to be on staff, what time her housemate came back, and that she wanted to be done before they got back. I was inwardly cheering—but I think Mum is having some adjustment experiences with Amber's new-

found voice. I reminded her that this is good ... we want Amber to be able to participate fully in life, and being vocal about her space was part of it. Mum agreed.

***Day 13:** Fun day today ... went to Amber's group home to do the final **Establishing Order** exercise. When we first showed up at her room I thought "UH OH!"—it was almost perfectly neat. There was practically nothing out of place. But then we opened the closet...and "BINGO!"—we spent two hours in her closet and it was totally organized when we left. At one point I asked her if she wanted to take a break and she said, "No, not now." This was contrary to any other time I've asked her.*

***Day 14: Relationship Concepts** went very well. Amber seemed quite interested. Mum said that Amber talked the ENTIRE drive to the office. She said that was a big change; in the past they would have driven quietly and listened to the radio. Mum said, "She's spent so much of her life not talking ... she has a lot to say!"*

***Day 15:** The rest of the concepts (we only had two left) went fine. Our celebration was great and I gave Amber a Certificate of Completion. During our meeting, Dad talked about how grateful he was for the changes they've seen already in Amber. He is thrilled and can't wait to see where this will take her. I reminded him that this is not the end ... in fact, it is the beginning ... as she begins to filter her future experiences through these new concepts.*

Case Study: An Adult's Experience, 18 Months Later

Davis Facilitator Christien Vos of the Netherlands worked with an adult male over the course of a year, seeing him once every two weeks. He struggled with the program and was often argumentative and resistant; however, after completing the program he has experienced profound changes in his life:

> At age 39, Willem, a high-functioning autistic male, lived alone and had no friends. When he came to me, he was unable to do more than one activity a day and repeatedly failing in getting or keeping a job. He was very suspicious and overly sensitive, and spoke with a stutter. He was also extremely bright, but lacked creativity.
>
> The Davis Autism Approach Program was a hard journey for him. He detested working with clay and questioned and resisted many of the concepts at the outset. Nonetheless, he continued to come to my office once every two weeks over the course of a year. Along the way, his aversion decreased, and our discussions were getting shorter and less offensive/defensive. He started to enjoy the feeling each mastered concept gave him.
>
> Because he lived alone, had no friends, and no job, it was difficult for him to get feedback in daily life. However, after a few months, while discussing his experiences in the weeks before, he was able to recognize the changes in his own thought processes and behavior.
>
> After he completed the program, I did not hear from him for some time. Finally, 18 months later, he contacted me by email and set up an appointment so that he could talk about his current life.

At that meeting he reported the following changes:

–he is not afraid of others anymore, although he still feels he is overly suspicious and he still stutters
–he has an overview in social situations, understands why people act the way they do, and is not feeling afraid, upset, angry, lost, or stressed out any more
–he can handle several things at the same time, and can handle multiple tasks in their proper sequence, staying relaxed and oriented
–he develops initiatives, and really executes them
–he has become more creative—for example, he has started to draw
–he is the team captain and webmaster of his bridge club, and writes reports of bridge tournaments for the bridge community
–he has joined a discussion group (in real life, not on the web) which meets regularly for dinner before their discussion
–he is making plans for his future

Case Study: A Child with Asperger's, One Year Later

Davis Facilitator Gale Long was also able to report the long-term changes of a young girl that she worked with. The child's mother also provided background information.

Kayla' mother reported:

Kayla had many of the symptoms of Asperger's Syndrome. Besides the speech issues, she struggled with rage and anger, was easily over stimulated by sounds, crowds, lights and smells. Her motor skills were underdeveloped, making normal activities such as bike riding and walking difficult. Her obsessions and compulsions were issues that made daily activities difficult. Social cues were missing, making it hard for her to read facial expressions, body language, and the rules of conversation. She tended to be overly friendly. She had unusual sensitivities to light, foods and touch. Her sensory integration disorders caused a need for therapy for several years. As with most autistic individuals, she had difficulty with transitioning when changing activities, as well as difficulty making and keeping friends.

We were in a state of constant stress during her elementary years. The school had no plan to help her. They did not know how to deal with her in the classroom. The students didn't know how to interact with her. They would make fun of her and, because she had no verbal skills, she would become physical with objects. She was expelled from school because of her behavior, and went to a special behavioral school in 4th grade. When entering middle school, Kayla was faced with chaos, anxiety, wanting to fit in, feeling rejected, having no friends, and being bullied. The professionals informed me that I needed to accept the fact that Kayla would never be better.

The facilitator reported:

At our first meeting, Kayla guardedly entered my office. She hid behind her mother slightly and clung to her hand as though, if she let go, something terrible might happen. But her curiosity was evident by the way she watched me through beautiful blue eyes and long lashes. As she began to become more relaxed in my presence, a giddiness took over her and she began to squeal and jump up and down. With obvious excitement, she shared some experiences with me, but I had so much difficulty understanding her speech that I had to pretend I knew what she had said.

Facilitator Observations—
One Year after Davis Autism Approach:

I recently met with Kayla for an after-school meal. As the students were dismissed from class, I noticed Kayla calmly walking down the sidewalk chatting and laughing with a friend. What a differ- ence! A little over a year ago, as I picked her up for our autism sessions, it was common to see the others bullying her or ignoring her in the play- ground. Many times, she had been crying. My heart ached for her as she struggled to fit into her world.

Today, Kayla has many friends who treat her as an equal. Kayla just recently took part in an over- night trip and a day of rafting. In previous years, she had never had a friend and didn't have the skills to take part in an overnight experience. So this was huge—being able to overcome fears and inadequate social skills to actually enjoy a wonderful day with friends! Kayla still struggles at times, but she has the tools and the ability to assess situations and respond appropriately. I have learned lessons from Kayla as she has taught me to understand how difficult things are from the autistic perspective.

As we ended our dinner together, I asked Kayla's mother if she could tell me three words to describe Kayla before her Autism Program. She replied: isolation, frustration, and sadness. The three phrases that she uses to describe Kayla now: hope, lightness in attitude, and joy.

I anxiously awaited Kayla's response to the same questions. She carefully thought about it and told me her three words from before: sadness, loneliness, and misery. Today she says she feels happy, included and confident.

Case Study: Reflections on the Three Program Phases

Davis Facilitator Cathy Dodge Smith offers recollections of experiences with several of her clients, and relates each to different phases of the Davis program:

*During the **individuation** part of the program, I begin to see glimpses of the real person behind the autism mask, or noise, during brief periods of what we call orientation, and what most people would likely refer to as being totally present. In the beginning, such moments are brief and fleeting. One must be very alert to catch them and respond.*

I had one little seven-year-old in my office who was not much interested in what I had in mind for our agenda. For over an hour, he wandered around, chatted incessantly, touched things, and was generally in his own world. Even though he did address me from time to time, or ask me questions occasionally, he was not much interested in my responses, often not even waiting for my reply. Finally, he stopped in mid-stream, came to my little table where I was waiting for him, and looked me in the eye and said clearly, "OK. What are we meant to be doing?" I told him what I wanted him to do, and he sat right down and did it. He was totally with me for about five minutes, and then got up and was "gone" again.

As individuation becomes more stable, the fleeting moments of orientation gradually expand, and the amount of time spent "gone" gradually is reduced. This is not something I am doing; it simply happens as the client becomes more comfortable being in an oriented state, and knows how to get there voluntarily.

*The next segment of the program, **identity development**, allows the individual to progress quickly (relatively speaking) through the stages of normal development that he has missed, in part or in whole, because of not being totally present in the real world. As we explore these concepts together, the real world becomes more and more known to the client.*

I was once working with a young woman (26 years old) on the concept of "time." When I talked about the earth rotating and us being on it, she looked up with a beautiful expression on her face, and said the she suddenly felt "OK" and more balanced and connected being on this earth.

I had a similar experience with a young man as he completed work on the concept of "sequence." He had never been able to follow even a simple sequence of steps, such as a written recipe, or a written note telling him how to go to the grocery store, buy one item, and get back home. The look on his face as he repeated the final mastery step for sequence was one of pure joy, delight, surprise, and peace.

*Once identity development has been completed, the last segment of the Davis program is **social integration**. Once more, it is awesome to witness the awakening of awareness to how relationships work. One young lad told me he "really needed this," because he had always been totally frustrated by the things he was expected to know, but never told. He discovered these are what are usually referred to as "unwritten rules" of social interaction. We spent delightful time together trying to think of such "unwritten rules," and writing them down!*

A New World of Possibilities

Individuals come to the Davis program seeking *change*. Parents of autistic children are hoping for changes in the way their child behaves and interacts with others. Older autistic individuals who seek help on their own are hoping for changes that will help them overcome barriers in their lives that leave them feeling frustrated or unhappy.

The Davis methods help by providing tools to enable the person to self-regulate and monitor his ability to focus attention, to reduce stress, and to control energy level. The use of these tools changes the way the person perceives and responds to his environment. The Davis program also provides a system of learning concepts that gives the person enhanced insight and understanding of his world and his role, both in managing his own life and interacting with others. With new knowledge and skills, the opportunity for further change is created. In the Davis framework, *knowledge + skills + opportunity* provide the individual with *ability*—but it is up to the individual to exercise the *control* and the *responsibility* that will effectuate change within his own life. For each person, the path may be different, determined by individual goals, interests, and talents.

"Once my identity began to develop and my memory began, my primary desire in life was to become a real human being. I could see that others were something that I wasn't. My primary task, from the beginning, was to find a way that would allow me to be 'normal,' or at least appear to be. If I could find my own way through this chaos and if I could provide a 'map' for others of my kind to follow, then there would be value in my existence. The Davis Autism Approach is my best effort at providing that map."

-- Ron Davis

Glossary

Terms Describing the Davis Program

Advanced Concept: a concept which encompasses all of the underlying root constructions and common concepts

Base Concept: a concept stemming from the way a person experiences a root concept

Basic Concept: a concept reflecting knowledge derived from a root concept

Common Concept: a concept that is derived from two or more constructions

Concept Mastery: a sequenced procedure using clay modeling to represent abstract concepts

Dominant Arrow: a clay arrow used to draw attention to one part of a clay model

Feeling Bubble: a loop of clay with one end attached to the chest of the model of self; the models within the loop represent mental images that give rise to emotions

Individuation: the process of developing consistency of perception resulting in a conception of self as a single unit, separate from others

Orientation: a state of mind in which mental perceptions agree with the true facts and conditions in the environment.

Root Concept: a concept based on a natural law

Simplest Form Model: a Concept Mastery model using very simple clay elements, such as clay balls and arrows, as the simplest way to represent the idea expressed

Thought Bubble: a loop of clay with one end attached to the head of the model of self; the models within the loop represent mental activity

Identity Development and Social Integration Concepts

Ability	knowledge, skill and opportunity to control
After	happening later
Agree	what is thought to be actual or real
Another	individual separate from self
Bad	not in support of survival
Before	happening earlier
Behavior	how one acts or conducts oneself
Belief	what is felt to be actual or real
Body	physical form
Change	something becoming something else
Cause	something that makes something else happen
Consequence	something that happens as a result of something else
Continue	remain the same
Control	ability to cause change

Disorder	things not in their proper place, and/or not in their proper position, and/or not in their proper condition
Effect	something that is made to happen
Emotion	self created energy
Energy	potential to influence
Experience	survive as changed
Force	application of energy
Good	in support of survival
Intention	urge to satisfy need
Knowledge	experience of being at effect
Lifeforce	the urge to be who and what "I" am
Mind	thought process
Motivation	urge to control
Need	something that satisfies want
Opportunity	having authority, time, place, and conditions to act
Order	things in their proper places, proper positions, and proper conditions
Others	individuals separate from self
Perception	external awareness
Relationship	interaction of one with another
Responsibility	ability and motivation to control
Right	an action in support of survival
Rules	regulations that establish boundaries of acceptable behavior
Self	me

Sequence	the way things follow each other in time, amount, size, arbitrary order, and importance
Skill	experienced in causing a desired change
Survive	continue as self
Thought	mental activity
Time	the measurement of change in relation to a standard
Trust	the feeling that another is equal to self
Understanding	experience of observing
Urge	the instinctual desire to seek pleasure and avoid pain
Want	urge to exist as
Wisdom	experience of being at cause
Wrong	an action not in support of survival

Bibliography

American Psychiatric Association. "Proposed Revision: A 09 Autism Spectrum Disorder." *DSM-5 Development.* January 26, 2011. http://www.dsm5.org/proposedrevision/pages/proposedrevision.aspx?rid=94 (accessed October 31, 2011).

Bacon, Alison M., and Simon J. Handley. "Dyslexia and reasoning: The Importance of Visual Processes." *British Journal of Psychology* 101 (2010): 433-452.

Baron-Cohen, Simon. 'Out of Sight or Out of Mind? Another Look at Deception in Autism." *Journal of Child Psychology and Psychiatry* 33, no. 7 (October 1992): 1141-1155.

Boucher, Jill, Francisco Pons, Sophie Lind, and David Williams. "Temporal Cognition in Children with Autistic Spectrum Disorders: Tests of Diachronic Thinking." *Journal of Autism and Developmental Disorders* 37, no. 8 (2007): 1413-1429.

Bruner, Jerome S., and Leo Postman. "On the Perception of Incongruity: A Paradigm." *Journal of Personality* 18 (1949): 206-223.

Chen, Eric. "Autism Speaks for itself: Lost on Planet Earth." May 31, 2009. http://iautistic.com/autism-speaks .php (accessed October 6, 2011).

Chen, Eric Y. *Autism & Self Improvement: My Journey to accept Planet Earth.* Singapore: Eric Chen Yixiong, 2007.

Courchesne, Eric, et al. "Neuron Number and Size in Prefrontal Cortex of Children With Autism." *Journal of the American Medical Association* 306, no. 18 (2011): 2001-2010.

Cytowic, Richard E. "Synesthesia: Phenomology and Neuropsychology." *Psyche* 2, no. 10 (1995).

Davis, Ronald D. "My Study of Disorientation." Burlingame, California, 1997.

———. *Nurturing the Seed of Genius (Facilitators Workshop Manual)*. Burlingame, CA: Davis Autism International, 2009.

———. "Red Dirt and Water." *The Dyslexic Reader*, 1997.

———. "The History of Concept Mastery and Symbol Mastery." *The Dyslexic Reader* 30, no. 1 (2003): 1-5.

———. "Waking Up: The Origin of Concept Mastery." *The Dyslexic Reader* 40, no. 3 (2005): 10.

Davis, Ronald D., and Eldon M. Braun. *The Gift of Dyslexia, Revised and Expanded: Why Some of the Smartest People Can't Read ... and How They Can Learn*. New York: Perigee Trade, 2010.

———. *The Gift of Learning: Proven New Methods for Correcting ADD, Math & Handwriting Problems*. New York: Perigee Trade, 2003.

Dawson, Michelle, Isabell Soulières, Morton Ann Gernsbacher, and Laurent Mottron. "The Level and Nature of Autistic Intelligence." *Psychological Science* 18, no. 8 (August 2007): 657-662.

Dawson, Michelle, Laurent Mottron, and Morton Ann Gernsbacher. "Learning in Autism." In *Learning and Memory: A Comprehensive Reference: Cognitive Psychology*, by J.H. Byrne and H. Roediger (Editors), 759-772. New York: Elsevier, 2008.

Dinstein, Ilan, et al. "Disrupted Neural Synchronization in Toddlers with Autism." *Neuron* 70, no. 6 (2011): 1218-25.

Farley, Adam, Beatriz López, and Guy Saunders. "Self-conceptualisation in autism: Knowing oneself versus knowing self-through-other." *Autism* 14, no. 5 (September 2010): 519-530.

Frith, Chris D., and Uta Frith. "The Self and Its Reputation in Autism." *Neuron* 57, no. 3 (February 2008): 331-332.

Frith, Uta, and Francesca Happé. "Theory of mind and self-consciousness: What it is like to be autistic." *Mind & Language* 14, no. 1 (March 1999): 1-22.

Gernsbacher, Morton Ann, Michelle Dawson, and Laurent Mottron. "Autism: Common, heritable, but not harmful." *Behavioral and Brain Sciences* 29, no. 4 (2006): 413-414.

Happé, Francesca. "Theory of Mind and the Self." *Annals of the New York Academy of Sciences* 1001 (2003): 134–144.

Hobson, R. Peter. "Explaining autism: Ten reasons to focus on the developing self." *Autism* 14, no. 5 (September 2010): 391-407.

Hobson, R. Peter. "On the origins of self and the case of autism." *Development and Psychopathology* 2, no. 2 (2008): 163.

Hobson, R. Peter, and Jessica A. Meyer. "Foundations for self and other: a study in autism." *Developmental Science* 8, no. 6 (November 2005): 481-491.

Hollander, Eric, et al. "Oxytocin Increases Retention of Social Cognition in Autism." *Biological Psychiatry* 61, no. 4 (February 2007): 498-503.

Jacob, Suma, Camille W. Brune, C.S. Carter, Bennett L. Leventhal, Catherine Lord Lord, and Edwin H. Cook Jr. "Association of the oxytocin receptor gene (OXTR) in Caucasian children and adolescents with autism." *Neuroscience Letters* 417, no. 1 (April 2007): 6-9.

Kamio, Y., and M. Tochi. "Dual access to semantics in autism: is pictorial access superior to verbal access?" *Journal of Child Psychology and Psychiatry* 41, no. 7 (Oct 2000): 859-867.

Kanner, Leo. "Autistic Disturbances of Affective Contact." *Nervous Child* 2 (1943): 217-50.

Kanner, Leo. "The Conception of Wholes and Parts in Early Infantile Autism." *American Journal of Psychiatry* 108 (July 1951): 23-27.

Kouijzer, Mirjam E.J., Hein T. van Schie, Jan M.H. de Moor, Berrie J.L. Gerrits, and Jan K. Buitelaar. "Neurofeedback treatment in autism. Preliminary findings in behavioral, cognitive, and neuro-physiological functioning." *Research in Autism Spectrum Disorders* 4, no. 3 (July-September 2010): 386-399.

Kouijzer, Mirjam E.J., Jan M.H. de Moor, Berrie J.L. Gerritsb, Marco Congedo, and Hein T. van Schie. "Neurofeedback improves executive functioning in children with autism spectrum disorders." *Research in Autism Spectrum Disorders* 3, no. 1 (January 2009): 145-162.

Lerer, E., S Levi, S. Salomon, A Darvasi, N. Yirmiya, and R.P. Ebstein. "Association between the oxytocin receptor (OXTR) gene and autism: relationship to Vineland Adaptive Behavior Scales and cognition." *Molecular Psychiatry* 13 (2008): 980-988.

Lind, Sophie E. "Memory and the self in autism: A review and theoretical framework." *Autism* 14, no. 5 (Sep 2010): 430-57.

Lind, Sophie E., and D.M. Bowler. "Delayed self-recognition in children with autism spectrum disorder." *Journal of Autism and Developmental Disorders* 39, no. 4 (Apr 2009): 634-50.

Lombardo, Michael V., and Simon Baron-Cohen. "The role of the self in mindblindness in autism." *Consciousness and Cognition* 20, no. 1 (March 2011): 130-140.

Lombardo, Michael V., et al. "Atypical Neural Self-Representation in Autism." *Brain* 133, no. 2 (2010): 611-624.

Lombardo, Michael V., Jennifer L. Barnes, Sally J. Wheelwright, and Simon Baron-Cohen. "Self-referential cognition and empathy in autism." *PLoS ONE* 2, no. 9 (2007): e88e.

Markram, Kamila, and Henry Markram. "The Intense World Theory—A Unifying Theory of the Neurobiology of Autism." *Frontiers in Human Neuroscience* 4 (December 2010): 224.

Meyer, Jessica A., and Peter R. Hobson. "Orientation in relation to self and other: The case of autism." *Interaction Studies* 5, no. 2 (November 2004): 221-244.

Mitchell, Peter, and Kelly O'Keefe. "Do Individuals with Autism Spectrum Disorder Think They Know Their Own Minds?" *Journal of Autism and Developmental Disorders* 38, no. 8 (Sep 2008): 1591-1597.

Mottron, Laurent. "Commentary: The Power of Autism." *Nature* 479, no. 5 (November 2011): 33-35.

Mukhopadhyay, Tito Rajarshi. *The Mind Tree: A Miraculous Child Breaks the Silence of Autism.* New York: Arcade Publishing, 2003.

Mundy, Peter, Mary Gwaltney, and Heather Henderson. "Self-referenced processing, neurodevelopment and joint attention in autism." *Autism* 14, no. 5 (September 2010): 408-429.

Pert, Candace B. *Molecules of Emotion: The Science Behind Mind-Body Medicine.* New York: Simon & Schuster, 1999.

Pineda, J.A., et al. "Positive behavioral and electrophysiological changes following neurofeedback training in children with autism." *Research in Autism Spectrum Disorders* 2, no. 3 (July-September 2008): 557-581.

Postman, Leo, and Jerome S. Bruner. "Perception Under Stress." *Psychological Review* 55, no. 6 (Nov 1948): 314-323.

Redcay, Elizabeth, and Eric Courchesne. "When is the Brain Enlarged in Autism? A Meta-Analysis of All Brain Size Reports." *Biological Psychiatry* 58, no. 1 (Jul 2005): 1-9.

Sahyoun, Chérif P., Isabelle Soulières, John W. Belliveau, Laurent Mottron, and Maria Mody. "Cognitive Differences in Pictorial Reasoning Between High-Functioning Autism and Asperger's Syndrome." *Journal of Autism and Developmental Disorders* 39, no. 7 (2008): 1014-1023.

Smith, Adam. "The Empathy Imbalance Hypothesis of Autism: A Theoretical Approach to Cognitive and Emotional Empathy in Autistic Development." *The Psychological Record* 59, no. 3 (2009): 489-510.

Soulières, Isabelle, et al. "Enhanced Visual Processing Contributes to Matrix Reasoning in Autism." *Human Brain Mapping* 30, no. 12 (Dec 2009): 4082-4107.

Soulières, Isabelle, Michelle Dawson, Morton Ann Gernsbacher, and Laurent Mottron. "The Level and Nature of Autistic Intelligence II: What about Asperger Syndrome?" *PLoS ONE* 6, no. 9 (2011): e25372.

Soulières, Isabelle, Thomas A. Zeffiro, M.L. Girard, and Laurent Mottron. "Enhanced mental image mapping in autism." *Neruopsychologia* 49, no. 5 (April 2011): 848-857.

Tammet, Daniel. *Born on a Blue Day: Inside the Extraordinary Mind of an Autistic Savant*. New York: Free Press, 2007.

Tau, Gregory Z, and Bradley S Peterson. "Normal Development of Brain Circuits." *Neuropsychopharmacology* 35, no. 1 (January 2010): 147-168.

Taylor, Jill Bolte. *My Stroke of Insight: A Brain Scientist's Personal Journey*. New York: Viking, 2008.

Teigeh, K.H. "Is a sigh "just a sigh"? Sighs as emotional signals and responses to a difficult task." *Scandinavian Journal of Psychology*. 49, no. 1 (2008): 49-57.

Toichi, Motomi, et al. "A lack of self-consciousness in autism." *American Journal of Psychiatry* 159 (August 2002): 1422-1424.

Uddin, Lucina Q. "The self in autism: An emerging view from neuroimaging." *Neurocase* 17, no. 3 (2011): 201-208.

Uddin, Lucina Q., et al. "Neural Basis of Self and Other Representation in Autism: An fMRI Study of Self-Face Recognition." *PLoS ONE* 3, no. 10 (2008): e3526.

van der Hoort, Björn, Arvid Gutertam, and H Henrik Ehrsson. "Being Barbie: The Size of One's Own Body Determines the Perceived Size of the World." *PLoS ONE* 6, no. 5 (2011): e20195.

Wellman, Henry M., David Cross, and Julanne Watson. "Meta-Analysis of Theory-of-Mind Development: The Truth about False Belief." *Child Development* 72, no. 3 (May/June 2001): 655-684.

Williams, David. "Theory of own mind in autism: Evidence of a specific deficit in self-awareness?" *Autism* 14, no. 5 (Sep 2010): 474-94.

Williams, David, and Francesca Happé. "Representing intentions in self and other: studies of autism and typical development." *Developmental Science* 13, no. 2 (Mar 2010): 307-19.

Wolff, Jason J., et al. "Differences in White Matter Fiber Tract Development Present From 6 to 24 Months in Infants With Autism." *The American Journal of Psychiatry*, February 2012: doi: 10.1176/appi.ajp.-2011.11091447.

Internet Resources

The Davis Autism Approach web site is here: **www.davisautism.com**

You can find the names and contact information for all currently licensed Davis Autism Facilitator/Coaches at **www.davisautism.com/contact_facilitator.html**

For information about research and developments of the Davis NOIT device for auditory orientation, see **www.noitresearch.org**

You can find more information about the Davis program for dyslexia, including current research reports, at **www.dyslexia.com**